Suggestions f

Set aside a regular time and p... ...ad and pray undisturbed. Before ... ...nd it helpful, use the BRF Prayer...

In *Guidelines*, the introduc... ...es or themes to be studied, wh... ...ly, weekly or whatever best fits ... ...u will need a Bible (more than one if you want to compare different translations) as Bible passages are not included. Please don't be tempted to skip the Bible reading because you know the passage well. We will have utterly failed if we don't bring our readers into engagement with the word of God. At the end of each week is a 'Guidelines' section, offering further thoughts about or practical application of what you have been studying.

Occasionally, you may read something in *Guidelines* that you find particularly challenging, even uncomfortable. This is inevitable in a series of notes which draws on a wide spectrum of contributors and doesn't believe in ducking difficult issues. Indeed, we believe that *Guidelines* readers much prefer thought-provoking material to a bland diet that only confirms what they already think.

If you do disagree with a contributor, you may find it helpful to go through these three steps. First, think about why you feel uncomfortable. Perhaps this is an idea that is new to you, or you are not happy about the way something has been expressed. Or there may be something more substantial – you may feel that the writer is guilty of sweeping generalisation, factual error, or theological or ethical misjudgement. Second, pray that God would use this disagreement to teach you more about his word and about yourself. Third, have a deeper read about the issue. There are further reading suggestions at the end of each writer's block of notes. And then, do feel free to write to the contributor or the editor of *Guidelines*. We welcome communication, by email, phone or letter, as it enables us to discover what has been useful, challenging or infuriating for our readers. We don't always promise to change things, but we will always listen and think about your ideas, complaints or suggestions. Thank you!

To send feedback, please email **enquiries@brf.org.uk**, phone **+44 (0)1865 319700** or write to the address shown opposite.

Writers in this issue

David Kerrigan is a former missionary to Asia and Baptist pastor. Until 2017, he was general director of the Baptist Missionary Society, now BMS World Mission. David wrote *Prince of Peace in a World of Wars* (BRF, 2018).

Matt Lynch teaches Old Testament and serves as academic dean at Westminster Theological Centre. He is the author of *Monotheism and Institutions in the Book of Chronicles* (Mohr Siebeck, 2014). He also co-hosts a podcast on biblical studies and theology (visit **onscript.study**).

Michael Parsons is minister for discipleship at Lechlade Baptist Church and has previously been a theology lecturer in the UK and Australia, and commissioning editor for Paternoster and The Bible Reading Fellowship.

Andy Angel is the vicar of St Andrew's, Burgess Hill. Previously, he taught New Testament in Church of England training colleges and has written *Playing with Dragons* (Cascade, 2014) and *Intimate Jesus* (SPCK, 2017).

David Walker has been bishop of Manchester since 2013, prior to which he served as bishop of Dudley from 2000. In 2015, he was awarded his PhD for his studies of Anglican belonging. David is a Franciscan tertiary.

Peter Hatton is a tutor at Bristol Baptist College, specialising in Bible and preaching. Before teaching in Bristol, he served for 25 years as a Methodist minister. He is convinced that those Christians who are seeking renewal and fruitful engagement with contemporary culture will discover the wisdom required for such a reformation in the pages of scripture.

Paul Bradbury is a pioneer minister based in Poole. He leads Poole Missional Communities, which works to animate new forms of church and works with CMS enabling pioneering across the south.

Helen Paynter is a Baptist minister, director of the Centre for the Study of Bible and Violence at Bristol Baptist College, and editor of BRF's *Guidelines* Bible reading notes.

Graham Dow was bishop of Carlisle for eight years, bishop of Willesden (London) and vicar of Holy Trinity Church (Coventry) for eleven years. He loves expounding the Bible, supporting Holy Spirit renewal and praying for healing, the liberation of lay ministry and God's purpose in daily work.

Fiona Gregson is part-time associate priest at St John's Harborne, Birmingham and splits her time between the church, teaching and caring for her young daughter.

Helen Paynter writes...

As I write this editorial, the EU elections of May 2019 are in full swing. Right-wing politicians are being 'milkshaked', and across Europe the 'gilets-jaunes' have been gathering momentum. Of course, by the time you read this, all sorts of political developments will have happened. But I doubt that one thing will have changed, or at least changed for the better. I doubt that public confidence in the governing authorities will be growing; I doubt that our trust in our political servants (or is it masters?) will have increased. How is the church to respond to such challenging times?

I'm very pleased that several writers have touched on this matter in this issue. Bishop David Walker begins his fortnight of reflections on 'Challenges 20:20' with a reflection on our relationship to the governing bodies. This theme is developed in more detail by the former bishop of Carlisle, Graham Dow, in a thought-provoking series of reflections on the relationship between church and state. David Kerrigan's engaging fortnight on 'Mission 20:20' discusses matters such as economics, the nature of human well-being and truth-telling: all themes that run deeply through our public discourse in this generation.

What else do we have on offer? Well, we have a rich and multi-voiced exploration of discipleship. Michael Parsons gives us a challenging week of reflections explicitly on this theme: 'When Christ calls a person, he bids them to come and die' (paraphrased from Dietrich Bonhoeffer). I'm also delighted that Andy Angel is continuing his tour through Matthew's gospel. In this edition, he invites us to consider the demanding claims that Jesus makes on his disciples, as we are led through Matthew 8—10. And, speaking of the tough call of discipleship, Fiona Gregson takes us through Philippians, penned from prison, in a fortnight of reflections that begins with the parts of Acts describing Paul's ministry in Philippi – also marked by a spell in prison, of course. As Andy Angel says, 'Jesus' challenges to his disciples echo his teachings more generally to all his disciples throughout time. His call to discipleship is never less than a call to total giving of ourselves in love and service.' Indeed.

To balance our focus on Matthew and Philippians, we also have some in-depth study of two Old Testament books. Matt Lynch takes us through 2 Chronicles, and I have the challenging task of leading us through the book of Joshua.

It is my prayer that our readers will be as blessed by these notes, as we have been in the preparation of them. May God use them to help guide us through these challenging times.

The BRF Prayer

Almighty God,
you have taught us that your word is a lamp for our feet
and a light for our path. Help us, and all who prayerfully
read your word, to deepen our fellowship with you
and with each other through your love.
And in so doing may we come to know you more fully,
love you more truly, and follow more faithfully
in the steps of your son Jesus Christ, who lives and reigns
with you and the Holy Spirit, one God forevermore.
Amen

Mission 20:20: mission and the kingdom of God

David Kerrigan

Jesus was crystal clear about the purpose of his life and ministry: 'I must proclaim the good news of the kingdom of God to the other cities also; for I was sent for this purpose' (Luke 4:43).

Today, as we participate in this mission, the establishment of the kingdom of God – or the kingdom of heaven (the meaning is the same) should be just as clear in our endeavours. Mentioned a combined total of 98 times in the New Testament, the kingdom of God is simply the rule of God on earth. It is the reason Jesus came.

This view has not always held sway. From Augustine to the Reformers, theologians typically equated the kingdom of God with the church. From the 19th century onwards, scholars thought of the kingdom more as God's reign in our hearts, a 'personal faith' emphasis. Today, we speak more readily of the kingdom being wherever the reign of God, or the lordship of Christ, is evident. We will look more closely at this below.

The Dutch theologian Abraham Kuyper (1837–1920) said, 'There is not a square inch in the whole domain of our human existence over which Christ, who is sovereign over all, does not cry, "Mine!"' It's a famous quotation and, over the next two weeks, it will take our studies in an unusual direction. After three foundational studies, we will explore seven areas of life where the lordship of Christ, rightly expressed, builds the kingdom of God. These areas are social media, science, well-being or health, commerce (in three parts), migration, education and evangelism. In each case, we ask, 'How is God's rule expressed here?'

Unless stated otherwise, Bible quotations are taken from the NRSV.

1 Mission, cross and resurrection

Acts 2:14–36

As we embark on these studies on mission and the kingdom of God, I want to address three elements that are of vital importance. Today, we look at the gospel itself and ask how the kingdom of God connects to it. Tomorrow, we look at the place of the local church in kingdom building, and the day after that we will reflect on ourselves and our role in this kingdom endeavour.

Today's reading takes us to the first sermon of the Christian church. We note what has gone immediately before: the ascension of Jesus in 1:6–11, making clear that Jesus' work on earth was complete, and the coming in power of the Holy Spirit in 2:1–13, making the mission of the church a reality.

Then Peter speaks of Jesus, and at the heart of his message is the proclamation that this man who was 'handed over to you according to the definite plan and foreknowledge of God, you crucified… But God raised him up, having freed him from death' (vv. 23–24).

This declaration is familiar for Christians. It's at the heart of the creed of the church and our life together: Christ crucified and risen. But it has the most profound importance for the mission we are called to share in.

The world in all its variety, beauty and ugliness unfailingly exhibits the corruption exemplified by the cross. In all the areas we shall explore in this series, we will be able to glimpse different ways in which something that is potentially good is not as it should be or as it could be. But we assert that the cross was the place of destruction of all that was – and is – corrupt.

How can we be so confident? Because of the resurrection! 'God raised him up, having freed him from death, because it was impossible for him to be held in its power' (v. 24) Here, then, is the paradigm for God's mission and our mission. The corruption of creation that characterises our fallen world has been utterly defeated at the cross. But the hope of the world lies in the resurrection of Jesus, 'Lord and Messiah' (v. 36), the prototype of the renewed creation to come. And it's that lordship that conveys the rule of Christ over every aspect of creation.

Of this 'all of us are witnesses' (v. 32), and we are blessed because, unlike Thomas, we have not seen or touched but we believe because of the gift of faith (John 20:29).

2 Mission and the local church

Peter C. Phan, a Vietnamese Catholic theologian, argues in his contribution to *Landmark Essays in Mission and World Christianity* that the next 50 years of the church will not see a new form of Christendom, but a new way of being the church. Phan argues that, in Asia at least, 'the kingdom of God and not the church [will be] the centre of the church's life and activities'. He goes on to say that 'no longer is the church the pinnacle or the centre of the Christian life… [but] the reign of God is installed as the ultimate goal of… the church'. In effect, he argues for a kingdom-centred church rather than a church-centred kingdom.

When Jesus conjures up a picture of the day of judgement, his focus is not on who is in the church, but on who bears the fruit of being a kingdom builder. Of course, Matthew 28:19–20 makes clear that we are to preach and baptise and make disciples, and disciples will come together with Christ in their midst (Matthew 18:20). This, at its simplest, is the church. But the church is there to repair, redeem or transform the world, not to hide away from it. We will call it away from sin, but we will also address the disease that sin has brought about. The hungry, the thirsty, the poor, the sick and the estranged are all in view in today's passage. But just as we might mentally consign this to simply 'doing good' (as if that were a low-value thing), Christ shocks us by saying that he is there in those he has described. He is there in the circumstances of human life where the reign of God is not visible.

Here, then, we set a template for our mission: God's people, called and gathered, with Christ in our midst, but that same Christ calling us into his world, where he invites us to be agents of his transforming mercy and grace. There is no churchless Christianity. Our adoption as sons and daughters finds expression when we are together. Our worship expresses our unity when we are together. We discern the mind of Christ through his word when we are together. But 'together' we dare not stay. Monday morning, as the sun rises, we are a missionary people headed for the schools and hospitals, the offices and shops, the neighbourhoods and laboratories where we work. God is building his kingdom there, and we're invited to participate.

3 Mission, truth and character

John 8:30–59

If a reputable plumber says the boiler needs changing, we usually trust them. If someone says, 'I love you', and we believe it, it will be because we trust them. Truth is linked to trust – trust in the truth teller. And trust is gauged by character – from one end of the spectrum, 'Is this person who they say they are?', to the other end, 'Is their life consistent with what they say?' Is my plumber qualified? Is my lover faithful? Is my pastor above reproach? Is my MP self-serving? Truth based on trust; trust evidenced by character.

In today's text, Jesus addresses those who have 'believed in him'. He encourages them to persevere 'in my word' (v. 31), to go on trusting him. The effect of such trust is profound – 'You will know the truth, and the truth will set you free' (v. 32, NIV). But here, they stumble. He declares that he knows their intention to kill him (vv. 37, 40). In spite of their plea to be children of God (v. 41), he condemns them as children of the devil, the father of lies (v. 44), full of deceit. Jesus compares their untrustworthy characters to his trustworthiness – 'Can any of you prove me guilty of sin?' (v. 46, NIV).

Mission is truth-telling in its various guises. Often, it is literally speaking of God our Father and the person and work of Christ. But implicitly, we are also asking people to trust us, and that decision will be based on who they see us to be. As a mission worker in Bangladesh, I needed to learn the language and culture as a way of communicating but also showing respect. I accepted hospitality, asked for forgiveness for my mistakes and tried to commend myself to others. Only then did my character, I hope, inculcate trust, and from that trust I pray that my witness, sometimes with words, was received.

Sometimes we can hide behind the line 'I don't have the gift of evangelism', but everyone is encouraged to become more Christlike (Ephesians 4:13). And a Christlike character commends itself to be trusted by others, and from that place we can live and speak the truth, however simply. I see in some a bold confidence in mission, and if I also see a consistent character, I rejoice. But if I see a charlatan, or someone whose life is not consistent with their message, I recoil. Messengers of the truth must have characters worthy of trust.

4 Mission and social media

I joined Facebook in 2008 and, having lived in many places during my life, I have found it overwhelmingly helpful for keeping in touch with friends and acquaintances. But social media has downsides, too. Not all outcomes are consistent with God's kingdom.

Today's well-known passage speaks of love, a reminder that the God of love we follow should shape all our social engagements, online or in person. Social media voices can be akin to 'clanging cymbols (v. 1) – all noise and discord. Social media can be hateful, whereas without love 'I am nothing' (v. 2). While love is patient (v. 4), social media usually isn't. On several occasions, I have posted something online and then deleted it; the ability to publish the first thing that comes into our minds isn't always a good thing.

Love is kind (v. 4), but social media often isn't. School-age children are particularly vulnerable as social media has become a platform for bullying of a most pervasive kind – following the child into the home and bedroom with no escape from the torment.

Love, we are told, isn't boastful (v. 4) yet we naturally tend to portray only the good things in our lives – smiling family occasions, significant achievements, selfie-worthy moments – and in the process we can become self-centred, over-preening or forgetful of the struggles of others. Love isn't arrogant, rude or insistent on having its own way (vv. 4–5) and, while social media can be a forum for the interchange of ideas, time and again it becomes a shouting place rather than a listening place.

At a deeper level, while love 'rejoices in the truth' (v. 6), social media has now been proven to be a vehicle for lies, false claims, fake news and propaganda that cuts to the very core of what it means to be human. Elections have been swayed through its influence such that we are in danger of losing the distinction between truth and falsehood, a trait that scripture lies at the feet of all that is evil (John 8:44).

In short, social media is one of the most powerful phenomena of our generation. We are social beings, created in the image of God, created for community and called to grow into maturity (v. 11). Our fullest engagement with God will be face-to-face (v. 12), a cautionary reminder that social media is a valuable form of human interaction, but one fraught with dangers. What does it mean to be a Christian presence on social media?

5 Mission and science

Today's Bible reading is unequivocal. Though the style is poetic, the message is clear: God is the all-powerful creator (v. 12), instructed by no one (vv. 13–14), awed by nothing (vv. 15–17) and beyond comparison (vv. 18–20, 25). Our knowledge of him is beyond our natural understanding (vv. 21–24). And yet, there is an affirmation, borne out in our own experience, that our eyes can see and our minds can grasp the wonders he has done (v. 26). Over centuries, science has made great leaps in our knowledge and understanding because the universe yields its God-given secrets. Science, at its peak, is a journey into the mind of God.

I find it hard to remember that in my childhood years of the 1950s and 1960s, we didn't have computers, the internet or mobile phones. According to the Office for National Statistics, life expectancy for men and women in the UK in 1900 was 48 years and 52 years, respectively. In 1960, it was 68 and 74. Today, it's 79 and 83. Science is largely responsible for these improvements, from childhood immunisation through to advances in the treatments of heart disease and cancers, and an awareness of the importance of nutrition and a healthy environment.

Along the way, we have had to grapple with the many ethical challenges that have emerged. Our ability to develop nuclear technology raised questions about the rightness of having, let alone using, nuclear weapons and the dangers of nuclear reactors to human life and the environment. Science has helped infertile couples with IVF treatment which, to most people, is seen as a positive development. But gene editing that offers the prospect of addressing inherited genetic disorders also raises concerns.

Artificial intelligence holds out the prospect of earlier, more reliable medical diagnoses, but we also face the danger of major decisions that affect our lives being taken on the basis of similar computer algorithms. Many jobs are already being outsourced to robots.

The Bible isn't a science book. It is a revelation of God's involvement in the emergence of all that exists and God's purposes to redeem it. God is the creator of life and, for that reason, life is precious. How it starts, how it ends and how it is lived matter to God and matter to God's people. We stand in awe of God alone. We stand as a critical friend in the face of scientific advances. That is part of our mission.

6 Mission and human well-being

Luke 8:40–56

We use the language of 'national treasure' loosely these days, often to refer to much-loved entertainers. One of our true treasures is the National Health Service, capturing as it does the fundamental human right to have access to health care. The Methodist leader Donald Soper, writing in 1960 at a time when the pre-NHS world was still a living memory, reflected that the NHS 'has meant a new life to those always on the edge of poverty and want, who no longer need fear illness and physical disability as the final and irreparable blow to their hopes and happiness'.

Today's reading highlights two cases of illness. Jairus' daughter was twelve years old and dying, and the woman with haemorrhages that had lasted twelve years was desperate for a cure. There are so many perspectives on these stories, but the most basic element is that Jesus healed these two sick people. Sickness was not, and is not, God's will. To heal the sick is to give expression to the truth that in God's kingdom, sickness has no rightful place.

In the 1980s, I was treasurer of a mission hospital in Bangladesh. The sick and dying came every day in large numbers, and when someone died, the cultural expression of their grief was often a pained, gut-wrenching howl that echoed along the corridors. Unsettling at first, indeed to the end, it spoke to me of the severity of the fracture in God's creation that takes place when sickness and death disrupt otherwise fruitful lives, especially young lives.

Being as healthy as we can be is important. Paul, describing our bodies as temples of the Holy Spirit, urges us to 'glorify God in your body' (1 Corinthians 6:19–20). This is a prompt to ensure that our bodies are as healthy as they can be. The harmful effects of cigarettes, alcohol or junk food need to be eliminated or at least carefully managed. Exercise is good for similar reasons.

But these things are not just personal issues – they are community and national concerns. We should never entertain a situation where access to health care, and increasingly social care, depends on your ability to pay. As health care costs rise with an ageing population and ever-greater medical advances made, more funds will be needed, and these should largely be borne by society together. That is an issue of justice, kingdom justice, and it's part of the mission of God.

Guidelines

- In the introduction at the beginning of the week, I quoted Abraham Kuyper's words about the extent of Christ's lordship. Did those words help you see why, unusually for Bible readings perhaps, we then focused on social media, science and health in the latter half of the week?

- In 'Mission and the local church', I introduced the concept of being a *kingdom-centred church* rather than a *church-centred kingdom*. Does this make sense? Which model is dominant in your local church, or is it a mix? What is the evidence for thinking as you do?

- If there was one area from this week that challenged you to change in some way, what was it? Is it an area that would motivate others in your church?

1 Mission and commerce: the value of money

Acts 16:11–40

The conversion of Lydia, a woman of substance who was 'a dealer in purple cloth' (v. 14), is significant in our understanding of wealth. The Bible never denigrates money, only the love of it (1 Timothy 6:10), the idolisation of it (Mark 10:17–22) and hypocrisy concerning its use (Mark 14:4–7). A church met in Lydia's home (v. 40) and women were amongst those who financially supported the ministry of Jesus (Luke 8:2–3). Money is good!

Money puts food on the table, clothes on our back and a roof over our head. It funds schools to educate our children, health workers to care for the needy and police to enforce the law. All of these contribute to a just society. In short, money is a most powerful tool with which to give expression to God's rule.

The problem is the inequitable distribution of money, and the mission of the church in this respect is to address the root causes of this injustice. I see no problem with the fact that some jobs pay more than others. Lydia evidently had wealth, had a home and enabled the church to meet there. I have no issue with the fact that some will accumulate great wealth through hard work and creativity while others will earn much less. What we cannot see as other than sinful is a structure whereby people are trapped in a cycle of poverty that robs them of a life that flourishes.

At one end of the scale, we pay some executives obscene salaries, reward failing leaders with payouts as they leave, and pay eye-watering bonuses to those who make money using *other* people's money and who get bailed out with *our* money when they fail. Routinely we elect politicians who promise to lower taxes. But tax cuts for the 'haves' mean poor schools, low-budget hospitals and too few social workers for the 'have nots'. As our economy changed from the 1970s onwards, outsourcing relatively low-skill jobs, little was done to help communities ravaged by job losses and needing to retrain in technical skills.

As a result, communities have become poor, and people who are poor often lack good education. Teachers are deeply committed, and parents will try too, but a broken system erodes the motivation to help children succeed because jobs are scarce or insecure and poorly paid. Without education leading to jobs that pay well, accommodation is substandard. Food is bought that fills the stomach but fails to nourish. Health suffers and people lose hope. God's kingdom-centred church must address these issues.

2 Mission and commerce: the responsibility of wealth

Proverbs 22

We used to be 'a nation of shopkeepers', but not these days. Today's commerce is ruled by multinationals with brands that are instantly recognisable across the globe. How, then, can the Bible help us when it was written in an age when trade and barter were the defining characteristics of the economy?

Proverbs 22 may have been written in a different age, but it still packs a punch as it distils the wisdom of God. Wealth is put in its place straight away – a good name is more important than a good bank balance (v. 1). Given that dignity is often the first casualty of poverty, we are reminded that we share the same humanity, each created in the image of God (v. 2). This begins to speak to the conscience of the wealthy (which probably includes us), for it is unacceptable to tolerate abject poverty. We are told clearly that the fear of the Lord is life's true riches (v. 4).

Verse 7 is a statement of fact – wealth puts us in a place of power over the poor and, as we know, power corrupts. To be in debt is to be owned by another – that is what slavery means. My church, like many up and down the country, supports the work of Christians Against Poverty (CAP). In weeks when a family in the town goes debt-free, we celebrate this with a rousing cheer, affirming afresh the multifaceted liberation offered by the gospel.

Wealthy people often talk the language of investment, so verses 8 and 9 should be simple to understand. If we sow seeds of injustice through our life decisions, we will reap a harvest of trouble down the line. But be generous, not just in our charitable giving but in our respect for others, and we will be rewarded.

Verse 16 underlines this. Oppressing the poor may yield short-term financial gains, but, we are assured, such a strategy 'will lead only to loss'. Power raises its head again in verse 22, knowing that some captains of industry oppress the poor or trample on the rights of others because they are vulnerable. Zero-hour contracts, avoidable factory closures and appalling working conditions, especially in emerging economies, violate the poor simply because they are poor. You and I may not be doing that, but when do we raise our voices on behalf of the oppressed? God is on their side (v. 23). We should be, too!

3 Mission and commerce: a just economy

Jeremiah 22:1–17

We won't easily find extended portions of scripture that describe a whole economic system that reflects God's kingdom values. But today's text from Jeremiah speaks subtly about economic power, and power – used or abused – defines a just economy.

This text is addressed to the powerful, to the king of Judah and those who attend him (v. 2). We may not think of ourselves as powerful, but if you have a steady income, a secure home and some money in the bank, you are comparatively well-off and that gives you power. Similarly, you may not be a monarch, but are you a business owner, someone who employs a part-time cleaner or someone with influence in a company? If so, 'hear the word of the Lord... act with justice and righteousness' (vv. 2–3).

In particular, you should have a special eye for the most vulnerable, 'the alien, the orphan, and the widow' (v. 3). Consider today's foreigners in our midst, maybe at the local car wash or nail bar, who might be victims of modern-day slavery. Orphans and widows in ancient times were at risk because of the absence of a male provider; while our economic models have changed, single-parent families continue to be at risk today. This has implications for how we see our staff or colleagues, friends or neighbours, but also how we assess the righteousness of government policies.

How we live has consequences. 'If you will not heed these words... this house shall become a desolation' (v. 5). Today, we seem less ready to see God as an interventionist in the affairs of nations, but God's judgement is to be taken seriously. Civilisations rise and fall, and it would not be absurd to suggest that the growing inequalities of today's world, even within our own nation, are sowing the seeds of our destruction.

Verses 11–17 speak directly to Shallum, son of King Josiah, about his unrighteousness, not least in making his neighbours work for nothing (v. 13) to accomplish his dishonest gain (v. 17). When we can buy a garment for a fiver, and throw it away after a couple of uses, are we remembering that the person who made it in a country far away is, in effect, working for almost nothing?

Does this all sound too political? Well, politics means the activities that govern the *polis*, the city – or the country – where we long to see the kingdom of God established. So, yes, the gospel is unashamedly political.

4 Mission and migration

Deuteronomy 10:12–22

Today's passage starts bluntly: 'What does the Lord your God require of you?' What follows can be distilled down to this: fear the Lord and follow his commands (vv. 12–13). We are reminded of God's great love for his people, Israel (vv. 14–16). Nonetheless, his love is not narrow or limited in any way. He is just and fair to all, including the stranger (vv. 17–18). And his love of the stranger is not simply a kindly disposition – it is intensely practical. He provides food and clothing (v. 18), and pointedly Israel is commanded to do likewise (v. 19).

There is hardly a town in the UK where the presence of migrants doesn't remind us that the world is on the move. Some come as refugees, fleeing war or persecution. Others are economic migrants, seeking a better life. Still others come as students or to work in areas where we have a huge shortage of people, such as in the NHS or as seasonal farm labour. Many are Christians and join our churches. Others are from different faiths and their 'otherness' can unsettle people.

Migration clearly isn't a simple issue. In biblical history, we see that Abraham, Isaac and Jacob were variously migrants and refugees. Israel was captive in Egypt and later Babylon, while Mary and Joseph fled persecution with their newborn child. In today's world, we support missionaries whom we expect to be able to go and live in other people's lands. We have sometimes supported our government in waging war in countries that then fall apart, but we wash our hands of the millions who consequently have no homes, jobs, schools or hospitals and risk their lives to reach safer shores.

Every country needs a fair immigration system, and we are naive if we think in today's world a permanent open door is viable for any nation. But we do have a mandate to love our neighbour, including when that neighbour is a stranger in our midst. We will also be committed to the bigger picture, that of justice, ready to ask why people are poor, why people are not safe, why people are living in a country destroyed by war. A just, peaceful and prosperous Syria, Afghanistan or Libya, insofar as it is within our nation's ability to shape these things, is a better solution than 'flee to our country and we will welcome you'. But migration at some level is here to stay. Our response should reflect the fact that we as God's people were also strangers in a foreign land (vv. 19, 22). Maybe we still are.

5 Mission and education

Luke 2:41–52

For Jesus to be able to teach at the age of twelve such that people were amazed at his answers (v. 47), he must have been taught well. We are also told that 'Jesus increased in wisdom and in years, and in divine and human favour' (v. 52), so his education continued. In today's world, we can think that the goal of education is simply to produce the next generation of workers for our economy. That's not unimportant, but Proverbs 16:16 reminds us: 'How much better to get wisdom than gold! To get understanding is to be chosen rather than silver.'

Many Christians are teachers, so how do they see their mission when they arrive at school on a Monday morning? Is it to be well-prepared, to be diligent workers and to be pastorally aware of children or colleagues in need? Yes to each of those. But hopefully, it's also to open the eyes of the soul in each young person and help them see the awesome nature of the world around us. That's a huge ask among all the jobs a teacher has to do, but it represents more of a mindset than a task. So physics can be a pathway into seeing the origins of creation. Economics need not just ask how globalisation benefits the rich, but whether it penalises the poor. Mathematics is a window into the order that is so observable throughout creation. Human geography is a way of glimpsing the interconnectedness of people everywhere on the planet, not least as we share the same ecosystem that keeps us alive.

Step into the world of the arts and we get something else – an opportunity to be creative, to produce music, make pictures, dance and write stories. Some will think of these times as less productive – same with sports – but that is to measure everything purely in economic terms. The purpose of education is to grasp the opportunities to become fully human, to glimpse the fingerprints of the creator at every opportunity.

But educating young people is never just a task for teachers. Parents have the primary role, because the home is the most important classroom in the world. This is where values and integrity are birthed, where an appropriate lifestyle is modelled and developed, where faith is shared and nurtured. Pray for our teachers, yes. But pray, too, for parents. Both are at the forefront of this mission field.

6 Mission and evangelism

Matthew 28

At last – evangelism! The climax to Matthew's gospel is for many people the quintessential mission-sending text, and understandably so. Christ has risen (vv. 1–7), and the women are first invited by the angel to 'come, see' (v. 6) and then told to 'go quickly and tell his disciples' (v. 7). Both dynamics are vital – come and see, then go and tell.

Later, Jesus appears among the disciples and he, too, sends them out. 'Go and make disciples,' he says. Not converts, not church attenders, not nice, respectable people – but disciples. A disciple will of course be converted and will be part of the local church – though we won't waste time on the nice and respectable bit. Respectability was never a requirement to follow Jesus!

A disciple is a follower, and our following of the master, as we have seen, will need to be worked out in our home, in our church and in our places of work. Now, maybe, we see why our exploration of commerce, social media, science, character and so on is relevant. Mission is not just the distribution of Christmas leaflets or the occasional Alpha course. It's a whole-life commitment, and it takes us into every facet of life with the transforming gospel of Jesus Christ.

So we will go and make disciples and baptise them. We will teach them 'to obey everything that I have commanded you' (v. 20) and model the need to turn from sin, but we will go on from these to bring spiritual babes to full maturity in Christ. We will teach our people the full spectrum of the gospel – let your light shine before others, leave your offering at the altar and be reconciled with your brother, be faithful to your spouse, love your enemy, don't store up treasure on earth, serve one master, don't be a worrier, don't judge others and don't be a hypocrite. And those are just from the sermon on the mount! Above all, above everything else, love God and love your neighbour.

Surely this is too much for anyone! Well, yes and no. Yes, we won't all be perfect disciples. But no, it's not too much, because 'I am with you always, to the end of the age' (v. 20). As we close these two weeks of studies, we are reminded that the Lord is with us at all times and in all places. He is with us because, ultimately, it is he who is building his kingdom.

Guidelines

- Did the studies this week strike you as too political, or too secular? What discomforted you about the studies? Or what has encouraged you?

- In your experience, why is it difficult to talk about money matters? Is it simply a 'national characteristic', as some suggest, or does our unease reveal something else?

- To what degree do you think your church, or visitors to your church, hear and understand the breadth of our gospel message?

FURTHER READING

Robert L. Gallagher and Paul Hertig (eds), *Landmark Essays in Mission and World Christianity* (Orbis Books, 2009).

Lesslie Newbigin, *The Gospel in a Pluralist Society* (SPCK Classics, 2014).

Vinoth Ramachandra, *Subverting Global Myths: Theology and the public issues shaping our world* (IVP, 2008).

Joshua Searle, *Theology after Christendom: Forming prophets for a post-Christian world* (Cascade Books, 2018).

Andrew Walls and Cathy Ross, *Mission in the Twenty-First Century: Exploring the five marks of global mission* (Darton, Longman and Todd, 2008).

2 Chronicles

Matt Lynch

1 Chronicles began its story with Adam (1:1). In the form of a genealogy (1 Chronicles 1—9), the author then weaves through the peaks and troughs of Israel's history until it reaches the story's first climax in the reign of David and Solomon (1 Chronicles 10—29). From Solomon to the exile, 2 Chronicles then follows the story of God and his people from the bright heights of Zion to the dark days of exile, until that glorious day when Cyrus of Persia released the exiles to return to rebuild the temple.

The first nine chapters of 2 Chronicles narrate the 40-year reign of Solomon, David's son. He assumes the throne without any political opposition (compare 1 Kings 1—2) and devotes himself almost entirely to the construction of the temple. The book's focus on the temple proves central as we press on in the story.

In chapters 10—36, we read the accounts of Judean and Israelite kings, but with a clear focus on Judah. This is because the story follows the fate of the Davidic line, and especially the way kings related to the temple. We read, for instance, that Ahaz closes the temple's doors and destroys the temple's vessels (28:24). For the Chronicler, rejecting the temple meant rejecting God. By contrast, Hezekiah and Josiah are temple restorers. Hezekiah reopens the temple after its closure (29:3), an act not recorded in Kings, and Josiah restores the temple after carrying out an extensive purification of the entire land (2 Chronicles 34—35).

Finally, Chronicles organises its story of Judah's kings according to a pattern of 'mini' exiles and returns. The temple and priesthood close during times of abandoning God and reopen when the people's hearts return to God.

As post-exilic readers of Chronicles looked back at their glorious past, they might have asked, 'Where is the great and powerful God of the past?' The returnees had no king, no standing army, a small fraction of their former land (in a province called Yehud), and they remained under the thumb of a foreign power (Persia). Things looked rather bleak! For Chronicles, the answer to that question was this: God's power and presence are known and experienced as the whole people of God gather in worship at the temple. In what follows, we'll explore the fascinating temple-focused story of Israel that the Chronicler wrote to encourage a demoralised and vulnerable people.

Unless stated otherwise, Bible quotations are taken from the NIV.

1 The puzzle of wisdom and wealth

2 Chronicles 1

2 Chronicles 1 begins with an account of Solomon's reign. God established the kingdom in his hands, and, unlike the account in 1 Kings 1—2, he does so without any opposition to Solomon's rule. The next part of the chapter presents us with a paradox. God appears to Solomon at night to offer him anything he wants. He requests wisdom *and not wealth*, which God commends and then proceeds to give him wisdom *and wealth*. We might ask, is the point simply that the *desire* for wealth is problematic, and that if we desire the right things God might reward us with wealth? There's something to that idea. Look at the words attributed to Solomon in Proverbs: 'Honour the Lord with your wealth… then your barns will be filled to overflowing, and your vats will brim over with new wine' (Proverbs 3:9–10).

But notice Solomon's actual request in Chronicles, which differs from the account in Kings (1 Kings 3:6–9). In Kings, Solomon's request for wisdom related exclusively to ruling as king. But in Chronicles, Solomon asks God to fulfil *now* the promises made to David about building the temple (v. 9). While related to ruling, his wisdom was to be focused on completing the temple David prepared (compare 2:11). For that, he would need considerable wealth. The next chapter seems to confirm this idea, since Solomon makes material preparations for the temple. That God-given wealth funded and benefitted generations of worship at the temple. And like Bezalel – the wise builder of the tabernacle – Solomon used his wisdom to build a temple that reflected God's glory (2:4–5).

But we can't leave this story without qualification. Chronicles leaves us enough detail to ask whether Solomon uses all his wealth for good. First, we hear that Solomon bought horses from Egypt (v. 16), something Deuteronomy explicitly forbids kings to do (Deuteronomy 17:16). It was like importing weapons from your enemy. Second, Solomon conscripts 153,600 workers for hard labour. Like Joseph – who saved the world from famine (Genesis 41:57) but also reduced Egypt to servitude (Genesis 47:20–21) – Solomon's building projects came at a cost (10:4). Hero projects often do. And so we might add that giving great wealth or labour *for God* should always correspond with care for others and human flourishing.

2 A temple great and wonderful

2 Chronicles 2

When Solomon begins building the temple, he sends a message to Hiram of Tyre that explains his motives and objectives. 'The temple I am going to build,' he says, 'will be great, because our God is greater than all other gods' (v. 5). The temple's own status communicated God's status. But not only that, the temple showed God's greatness *over the gods*.

According to Psalms, the nations' gods are blind, deaf, mute and inactive, and those who worship them become like them (Psalm 115; 135). By contrast, Yahweh is living and active. Psalm 135, which many scholars think was composed around the time of Chronicles, says, 'I know that the Lord is great, that our Lord is greater than all gods' (Psalm 135:5). Chronicles seems to have this text in mind when Solomon claims that '*the temple* will be great, because *God* is greater than all the gods'. In other words, if the temple was spectacular enough, it could show Israel and the nations that Yahweh was a superior god. Temples were known in the ancient world to communicate a god's attributes.

But Solomon also knows the risks of trying to align God too closely with the temple. His father David learned that lesson when he first tried to bring the ark to Jerusalem. He didn't initially follow the Torah's requirements (1 Chronicles 13:7; compare Deuteronomy 10:8), and one man ended up dead (1 Chronicles 13:7–12). God wasn't going to play by David's rules, or let David co-opt the divine throne for his own political purposes. Similar risks beset Solomon's temple project. Building a temple might suggest that God can be confined. It might suggest that God is *only* a god for Israel. So Solomon continues, 'But who is able to build a temple for him, since the heavens, even the highest heavens, cannot contain him? Who then am I to build a temple for him, except as a place to burn sacrifices before him?' (v. 6).

This raises key questions. Could the temple effectively communicate God's greatness without reducing God? And could the temple convey *God's* greatness without simultaneously – and perhaps conveniently – becoming a tool of the royal house? Here at the start, Solomon wants to say, 'Yes!' The temple was not a mute idol that reduced God. It was more like an icon, meant to point beyond itself while also giving the people a way of engaging with the greatness of Israel's God.

3 A temple beyond history

Chronicles uses Kings as a source for retelling the story of the temple's construction (compare 1 Kings 6–7). God chose Solomon to build the temple, and Solomon does so (alongside the construction of his own palace). However, several noticeable differences from Kings appear, and they tell us something important about how the Chronicler wanted their readers to understand the temple.

First, the temple is located where Abraham bound his son Isaac on Mount Moriah (3:1; Genesis 22:2). This lends the temple historical and spiritual significance. Just as the 'angel of Yahweh' appeared to Abraham on Moriah (Genesis 22:11, 15), so also the angel of Yahweh appeared to David at the threshing floor of Ornan on Moriah (1 Chronicles 21:20–21). Second, and reaching back to our previous chapter, the temple was designed and built by a master craftsman who possessed 'wisdom and understanding' (2:12–13, my translation). The tabernacle was built with the same (Exodus 35:31). Third, the temple stood far higher than Kings suggests. Chronicles claims that the temple's vestibule reached 120 cubits, or 55 metres (3:4)! In Kings, the temple was only 30 cubits (1 Kings 6:2–3). Fourth, the altar was a massive 20x20x10 cubits (4:1), which Kings never mentions. Finally, Chronicles reports that the temple had ten tables of showbread (4:7–8, 19), whereas Kings reports one (1 Kings 7:48).

These differences are hardly accidental. And they shouldn't be understood in terms of Chronicles simplistically falsifying history. Chronicles knew its readers could access Samuel–Kings. Instead, Chronicles was telling its readers that the temple was to be truly 'great, because our God is greater than all other gods' (2:5). While the nations' gods could not see, hear, smell, taste or speak, Yahweh's eyes and ears were always open to prayers towards the temple. And his name would always remain there (7:15–16). For those who returned from exile and only saw a pitiful temple (Ezra 3:12;

Haggai 2:3), the Chronicler's account provided them with a source of historical pride. But it also pointed towards a future greater than the past. In the words of Haggai to the returnees, '"The glory of this present house will be greater than the glory of the former house," says the Lord Almighty' (Haggai 2:9).

4 Divine appearances and danger

2 Chronicles 7

Chronicles continues to walk the knife-edge between saying that 'God is *here* in *this* temple' and saying, 'Don't you dare try to contain God!' We notice in chapter 7 that immediately after Solomon's prayer, 'fire came down from heaven and consumed the burnt offering and the sacrifices, and the glory of the Lord filled the temple' (7:1). None of this detail appears in Kings, reinforcing the point that Chronicles cared deeply about the way God's presence validated the new temple (think of the divine messenger on the threshing floor).

Verse 3 then reports that the glory of the Lord was '*above* the temple' for all the people to see. This was not just a scene for priests; it was for everyone. As the people saw God's powerful presence, they knelt down and exclaimed: 'He is good; his love endures forever.' In other words, the congregation and priests respond to God's presence by uttering (in condensed form) the self-declaration of Yahweh that he gave to Moses on Sinai when he appeared to him in glory (Exodus 34:6–7). God's glory and loyal character are two sides of the same coin.

After a huge 14-day party, Solomon dismissed the people and found himself alone with God: 'The Lord *appeared* to him at night' (v. 12), the Chronicler tells us, evoking the last time that he and God were alone and Solomon asked for wisdom (1:7). This is the fourth major divine appearance in just seven chapters, but this one is different and carries with it a word of warning. God tells Solomon that he will *always* be available to his people if they seek him in prayer (vv. 14–17). However, if Solomon or his descendants abandon him for other gods, they will be exiled and God will reject the temple. God loved his magnificent home. It reflected his glory and greatness. He was present there. But he would not abide with disloyalty, and he would not commit his holy and good presence to the temple unconditionally. This must have been a sobering word for Solomon. And it proved to be a word that future kings would fail to heed.

God isn't afraid to bring hard warnings into the middle of this incredible celebration, if only to remind us that with great success comes the temptation to become proud, and even autonomous from God.

5 Daily rhythms of worship and obedience

2 Chronicles 8

Great experiences of God's presence are often followed by times of spiritual depletion. For instance, after the dramatic experience of God's fiery presence and victory over the prophets of Baal (1 Kings 17), Elijah found himself on the run, exhausted, frustrated and in need of sleep (1 Kings 18). Gerald Coates, founder of the Pioneer church network in the UK, is reported to have said, 'We have to make sure that these times of refreshing don't knacker us out altogether!'

2 Chronicles 8 moves us from the sublime to the ordinary. Without denying his powerful presence, God also knows the need for daily rhythms, seasonal celebration and regular duties before God. After telling us of Solomon's other building projects (vv. 1–11), Chronicles describes Solomon setting up burnt offerings for each day and for sabbaths, new moons and festivals (vv. 12–13) and appointing priests and gatekeepers for service at the temple (v. 14). All of this was in keeping with the law of Moses and the worship David established.

Only after setting up daily worship does Chronicles state: 'So the temple of the Lord was finished' (v. 16). This wasn't the end so much as it was a beginning. Now Israel could take up the vision of Moses and David and worship the God who was present.

Curiously, however, that vision didn't include daily dramatic appearances from God. Instead, that vision involved a future with daily praise, the daily giving of one's resources in sacrificial worship and daily attentiveness to the running of God's house. Eugene Petersen refers to the need for 'a long obedience in the same direction' in an instant society. For Chronicles, Israel needed a long obedience shaped by the laws of Moses and the instruction of David. From his meeting with God, Solomon knew that Israel's future depended on it.

The vision of daily worship and a long obedience is far less glamorous than the dramatic appearance of God's presence. Many Christians spend their lives chasing the next dramatic appearance, waiting for God's power to come with great fanfare. God sometimes chooses the sensational, but often simply calls us to meet him in the quiet and obedient rhythms of daily worship and commitment. Both sustain and empower us.

6 A new pharaoh

2 Chronicles 10

This chapter shows us that we were not wrong to detect trouble around Solomon's vast accumulation of wealth. Like many great monuments throughout history, such as St Peter's Basilica (funded by indulgences), Solomon's awe-inspiring projects came with a hefty price tag. After his death, rebellion broke out.

We read in 2 Chronicles 10 that the people called on Jeroboam (who had fled from Solomon to Egypt, of all places) to host a meeting with Rehoboam, Solomon's son, who was now king. They wanted to renegotiate the terms of their employment, which they considered unfair and burdensome (vv. 2–4). Rehoboam initially seems to listen, since he goes away to consult with the elders (v. 6). The elders suggest easing the people's workload. If he did, they argued, the people 'will always be your servants' (v. 7).

However, after consulting them, he then asks the 'young men who had grown up with him and were serving him' (v. 8). These were the cut-throat investors who believed that maximising profit and power depended on squeezing maximum work from labourers and establishing control. As if Solomon hadn't accumulated enough wealth! Rehoboam takes their advice and warns the people: 'My father scourged you with whips; I will scourge you with scorpions' (v. 14). This was clearly a ruler who had nothing but disdain for his people.

The plan backfires spectacularly. Once the people learn of Rehoboam's intransigence, they take action. Rehoboam was like a new pharaoh to the Israelites, so they appoint Jeroboam as a new Moses to liberate them from Rehoboam's rule. The people of Israel (the ten northern tribes) declare their independence: 'What share do we have in David, what part in Jesse's son? To your tents, Israel! Look after your own house, David!' (v. 16). From then on, Israel separated from Judah, and the kingdom split in two. Chronicles reminds the reader that these events were in keeping with the words of Ahijah the prophet (v. 15), though it is only a dim source of comfort as the people edged toward civil war (11:1–4). Mistreating others eventually comes back to haunt those in power.

Guidelines

This week focused on the rule of King Solomon and the division of the kingdom under his son Rehoboam. Chronicles focuses on Solomon's wisdom for temple building, his actual construction of the temple and the temple's dedication. We explored two theological tensions that Chronicles explores. First, we saw that God blesses his people with great wealth. But that wealth is meant for human flourishing and divine glory, and not self-aggrandisement. Second, we observed the tension between affirming God's presence in a place and recognising that God cannot (and will not) be limited or confined. You might consider ways that blessings come with responsibility, and ways that we are meant to guard against trying to manage God's power and presence.

1 Humbled

2 Chronicles 12

Rehoboam's pride and foolishness led Israel to split from Judah. With a reduced nation (now just Judah and Benjamin), Rehoboam set about strengthening himself militarily and financially (2 Chronicles 11). He fortified the border cities in Judah (the southern kingdom) and rebuilt ruined cities. The Levites from northern cities came south to serve at the Jerusalem temple, and the whole priesthood became strong and remained loyal to Rehoboam (11:13–17). Things were looking up.

2 Chronicles 12 hits us with another dose of reality. It reminds us that good kings rarely last. In fact, Chronicles consistently reports that kings crash to the ground at the height of their power. 'Pride goes before destruction,' says the sage (Proverbs 16:18). Rehoboam and the people 'abandoned the law of the Lord' (v. 1). As a result, the prophet Shemaiah says that God will 'abandon' Rehoboam to the power of Pharaoh Shishak (v. 5). The prophet implies that if the king wants to play at being pharoah, he will die at the hands of one.

But remarkably, Rehoboam and the leaders humble themselves. Because of this, God says he will *not* utterly destroy them (vv. 6–7). This follows a pattern we see with some consistency in scripture:

1 Sin
2 Announcement of judgement by a prophet
3 Opportunity to humble oneself
4 Yahweh turns from his decreed promise.

Before those who humble themselves, God often responds with mercy (compare Jonah). This means that while God's initial word is always serious, it is always spoken within the context of a covenant relationship between God and his people. And God takes the words and actions of his covenant partners seriously. As a consequence, the king's or people's abasement can change the course of his actions, as we see throughout the book of Chronicles. We'll come across this theme of repentance again, but for now it's worth noting its key role in this story.

But repentance demands permanent changes, which Rehoboam fails to make. For Chronicles, Rehoboam's chief failure boils down to this: he 'had not set his heart on seeking the Lord' (v. 14). He humbled himself when he faced disaster, but his turn from evil did not go far enough. After repentance, there is constructive work to be done. Our journey with God is not just about repentance. It involves actively seeking the Lord through worship, the pursuit of justice and wise leadership. Rehoboam ends up as a contradictory figure. He was a brutal leader who humbled himself, but failed to make lasting changes that would direct his heart towards God in worship.

2 Worship in battle

2 Chronicles 13

Abijah succeeds his father Rehoboam as Judah's king. Chronicles reports that Abijah prepares for war against Israel, but has only half the troops of his northern neighbour. However, in what appears to be a pre-emptive incursion, Abijah and his troops advance to Mount Zemarim, well into Israelite territory. From there, Abijah stands atop the mount and gives a speech not recorded in Kings. The scene is reminiscent of the speeches kings might give their troops before battle, like Aragorn's speech at Mordor's Black Gate or William Wallace's speech before fighting the English at the Battle of Falkirk.

However, Abijah makes no attempt to embolden his own troops for battle. Instead, Abijah indicts the north for their rebellion against the house of David (vv. 4–12).

It might seem strange that Chronicles would favour such hostility towards the north, especially when Judah was to blame for the split. However, Chronicles is concerned with the deeper spiritual rebellion of the north. In their hostility towards Rehoboam, the people had also abandoned the temple and the covenant (v. 5). Perhaps the people had a legitimate grievance with Rehoboam, but that does not necessarily legitimate Jeroboam's coup. Abijah points out that while Israel had more troops, they had weakened themselves but abandoning the Levites and priests (v. 9). They had cut themselves off from their life source.

By contrast, Judah had not abandoned the Lord, but worshipped him 'every morning and evening' with burnt offerings and incense in Jerusalem (vv. 10–11). This reminds us again that Judah found its true strength in worship. As if to reinforce this point, the narrator then reports that, as Judah charged into battle, the priests 'blew their trumpets and the men of Judah raised the battle cry' (vv. 14–15). In response, God routed the enemy. From this point on, Chronicles is a story of Judah, with only brief mentions of the north.

This priest-led battle scene evokes similar events in the battle of Jericho, where priests led the people of Israel in victory (Joshua 6). Likewise, as Judah devoted itself to worshipping Yahweh alone, it would win against numerically superior enemies (compare 2 Chronicles 20). In our day, the enemies we face may not be military in nature, but our need for loyal worship remains just as vital. We see that Jesus squared off against Satan by insisting on the need to 'worship the Lord your God and serve him only' (Luke 4:8; compare Deuteronomy 6:13). Jesus' example, and the example of Abijah, reminds us that worship is not just about singing. It is about aligning ourselves politically with God's advancing kingdom as it confronts real enemies.

3 Seeking God

2 Chronicles 15

If there's a phrase that captures the heart of Chronicles, it is this simple one: 'Seek the Lord.' The royal narratives begin by telling us that Saul did not seek the Lord (1 Chronicles 10:13–14) but instead sought spiritualists. By contrast, David sought God by taking care of the ark (1 Chronicles 13:3–14), and then instructing the Levites to seek the Lord (1 Chronicles 16:11, my translation): 'Petition YHWH and his strength, seek his face constantly.'

The emphasis on seeking God continues through the David and Solomon narratives (for example, 1 Chronicles 28:9; 2 Chronicles 7:14) and forms a kind of drumbeat for the book's account of royal history. Seeking Yahweh is Israel's only hope in times of war and peace.

But what does it mean to seek God? Chronicles puts flesh on the idea in two primary ways. First, seeking is an act of desperation. When trouble hits, the people cry out to God (not idols). We might call that the 'distress signal'. Asa cried out to God in distress, and God routed the Cushites (14:11–13). But secondly, there's a need for long-term pursuit of God through covenanted obedience. We might call that the 'theme music'. This kind of seeking is 'the filial spirituality proper to children of the covenant' (Hahn, p. 152). It involves loyalty to the Davidic covenant through regular worship of Yahweh. This second kind of 'seeking' is what Chronicles really wants to instil. How can we move from seeking God in moments of distress towards letting the pursuit of God form the theme music of our lives?

So after encouragement from Azariah, the people made a covenant to 'seek the Lord, the God of their ancestors, with all their heart and soul' (v. 12). This verse echoes the Shema, prayed daily by Jews to this day and described by Jesus as the heart of the law (Deuteronomy 6:4–5; Mark 12:30). The law was meant to shape a people whose entire lives were devoted to Yahweh alone. As the people promised to seek Yahweh, they pledged their loyalty with 'loud acclamation, with shouting and with trumpets and horns' (v. 14). As if to drill it into our minds, Chronicles states that because the people 'sought God', they enjoyed peace all around (v. 15).

4 A tale of two kings (Uzziah and Ahaz)

2 Chronicles 26; 28:16–27

Our two stories for today focus on the temple. In the first case, we learn of Uzziah, a king who dared to enter the temple (2 Chronicles 26). Uzziah reigned for 52 years. Like David, Solomon and Asa before him, he 'sought God'. But he did so only 'during the days of Zechariah', the high priest (26:5). It seems that the high priest often held the king in check (24:2). But after Zechariah's death, Uzziah became so proud that he waltzed into the temple to offer incense on the altar that stood in the holy place (26:16). Only the priests were to enter the holy place (26:18). For a king to enter was to commit *ma'al*, or violation against the divine realm.

God responded swiftly by afflicting Uzziah with leprosy on his forehead (26:19). To be leprous in or near the temple was strictly forbidden, so he was in a dangerous state (compare Leviticus 13:46). Seeking God involves humble submission to his authority, especially for those in positions of power, and especially when experiencing success or prosperity. Uzziah ended up a leper until the day of his death and was buried in a field in Jerusalem (26:21–23).

In our second story, we learn of Ahaz, a king who closed the temple (28:16–27). King Ahaz took an opposite, and even more dangerous, approach. 2 Chronicles 28:23 tells us that 'he offered sacrifices to the gods of Damascus, who had defeated him' (see verses 5–15). He worshipped the gods of apparent success – a short-lived approach, since Assyria soon defeated Damascus (compare 2 Kings 16:10). Then Ahaz took the bits and pieces left in the temple, shut its doors and built high places of worship to other gods throughout the land of Judah (28:24–25). He was 'utterly unfaithful' (*ma'ol ma'al*) against Yahweh (28:19, my translation), and so he died utterly disgraced. He was not even buried in Jerusalem (compare 2 Kings 16:20).

Ahaz was fascinated by the power of nations, but utterly unimpressed with God. He closed the temple of Yahweh and opened Judah to other gods. If we recall the words of Solomon from 2 Chronicles 2:5, Ahaz's actions become all the more egregious: 'The temple I am going to build will be great, because our God is greater than all other gods.' Ahaz typifies disdain for the temple and hastened Judah's slide towards exile.

5 The great Passover celebration

2 Chronicles 30

Hezekiah is a beacon of light among the latter kings of the Davidic line. Other than David and Solomon, Chronicles devotes the most attention to this Judean king. Not only did he do 'what was right in the eyes of the Lord', but he reopened the doors of the temple that his father Ahaz had closed (29:1–4). The Chronicler credits Hezekiah with reunifying Israel after the north's fall to Assyria, reforming worship, accumulating great wealth and, most significantly, for hosting a great Passover celebration. Doing so signalled that even after years of failure, new beginnings were possible.

2 Chronicles 30 begins with Hezekiah sending out Passover invitations to all Israel, including those in the north who had been alienated from Judah after their incorporation into the Assyrian empire (vv. 1–2). Passover commemorated the people's departure from Egypt and journey towards Sinai. While the Israelites weren't all in exile (some were; compare 2 Chronicles 28), they had been out of touch with God during Ahaz's reign. Thus Hezekiah and the leaders urged the people to 'return to the Lord' (v. 6) and 'come to his sanctuary' (v. 8). If they did so, they urged, 'he will not turn his face from you' (v. 9).

Once it got rolling, Hezekiah's Passover was a party to remember. In fact, the celebration was so great that the people extended it an additional seven days beyond the initial seven (v. 23). Most memorable, however, is the unity that this party demonstrated. With 'great rejoicing' (v. 21) all Judah partied, along with remnants from the north, Levites, priests and foreigners, (v. 25). Such joy was not had in Israel since the days of David and Solomon (v. 26). The chapter captures the book's vision of joyful worship by *all* Israel and foreigners around the temple in Jerusalem (v. 8). Israel's strength, hope and future depended on such worship. Verse 9 shows the importance of such unified worship. If the people would turn to God at the temple, even their brothers and sisters in exile would find mercy before their captors. This would have been a great source of comfort to Chronicles' post-exilic readers who gathered around the Jerusalem temple to worship. The story also reminds us of a simple yet profound truth that repeats like a chorus throughout the book of Chronicles: worship of God brings deep joy, for it reminds us of his covenant love and mercy (compare 1 Chronicles 16:34; 2 Chronicles 5:13).

6 The fall of Judah and hope of return

Chronicles doesn't dwell long on Judah's march towards exile. Like Kings, it tells the story in a rather matter-of-fact way. Once Josiah died, Judah's fate was in the hands of its Babylonian overlords. But there are several differences from the parallel account in 2 Kings 25 that clue us in on the Chronicler's concerns.

First, Chronicles suggests a link between the exile of Jehoahaz, Jehoiakim and Jehoiachin to Egypt and Babylon and the exile of the articles from the temple. The implication here is that the restoration of the temple was bound up with the restoration of the Davidic house (vv. 1–7, 10).

Second, Chronicles reports that the last Judean king (Zedekiah) failed to humble himself before Jeremiah the prophet (v. 12). This contrasts with Manasseh, who, despite his extreme wickedness, humbled himself and found favour with God when exiled (33:12; compare 33:23). Chronicles wants its readers to know that God continually extends opportunities to repent because he is merciful (vv. 15–16). But rather than soften his heart, Zedekiah 'became stiff-necked and hardened his heart' (v. 13). Perhaps most relevant for Chronicles, the people and priests were 'defiling the temple of the Lord, which he had consecrated in Jerusalem' (v. 14). Eventually, God had enough. He is slow to anger, but he does grow angry. He brought the Babylonians against Judah. They swept in, plundered the temple (v. 18) and burned it to the ground (v. 19).

Third, exile needed to be framed theologically. The exile was a tragedy, but not only that. It also gave the land its much-needed sabbath rest (v. 21). Evoking Jeremiah's prophecies (Jeremiah 25:12; 29:10), Chronicles reports that the land rested for 70 years. If calculated from the death of Josiah in 609, when Chronicles may have begun the clock, the exile would end in 539, when the Judeans returned to the land. The end of the land's 70-year sabbath rest came with a call to pick up trowel and hammer, 'go up' to Jerusalem and help rebuild (v. 23).

This is a fitting end to Chronicles – the last book in the Hebrew Bible. The book began with Adam (1 Chronicles 1:1) and ends with a summons. There's always hope beyond exile. As with Israel's exodus from Egypt, that hope is about more than liberation *from* oppression; it's liberation *into* a worshipful encounter with the living God, whose presence is available to all who seek him.

Guidelines

Chronicles begins with Adam and culminates in a call to return to Jerusalem and help rebuild the temple. For Chronicles, worshipping Yahweh is the way that humanity recovers its purpose and identity in the world. If Israel is meant to be a 'new Adam', they – and especially their kings – have to apply their wisdom to seeking God's presence. Insofar as they turned away from that path, they slid inexorably towards exile. But even in their darkest hour, Chronicles reminds the people that repentance is possible. Repentance is not just a one-time event, however. It involves a life of seeking God through a life of joyful worship. As we read about the past, Chronicles keeps directing us towards rhythms of life captivated by a God who keeps his covenant and is worthy of all praise.

FURTHER READING

Mark J. Boda, *1–2 Chronicles (Cornerstone Biblical Commentary)* (Tyndale House Publishers, 2010).

Scott W. Hahn, *The Kingdom of God as Liturgical Empire: A theological commentary on 1–2 Chronicles* (Baker Books, 2012).

Sara Japhet, *I & II Chronicles: A commentary (The Old Testament Library)* (Westminster John Knox Press, 1993).

Peter J. Leithart, *1 & 2 Chronicles (Brazos Theological Commentary on the Bible)* (Brazos Press, 2019).

Discipleship 20:20

Michael Parsons

'Discipleship' is one of those buzzwords which the church today is talking about whenever it has the opportunity. Several of the major denominations are reconsidering what it means to be a disciple of Jesus Christ in this very complex and fast-moving 21st century; many books are written on the subject. It's clearly important. And, yet, the word doesn't appear in the New Testament at all. So to glean its meaning, we need to start with Jesus' practice of calling disciples to himself and prayerfully ask the Lord to show us what this might mean for us today.

The following brief notes simply scratch the surface of some key texts and single out what I think are some of the main things we need to be thinking about today: Jesus, taking up our cross, gaining everything in him, the centrality of love, the significance of the Christian community and such like. These are foundational themes upon which we might build our view. There are many areas we haven't space to consider and some of these are significant, such as the work of the Holy Spirit.

As you reflect on these notes, consider carefully your own concrete situation – your personal call to follow Jesus, your Christian community and the task ahead of you. Pray for understanding, vision and the Spirit's resources, that you might reflect something of what the Lord calls you to.

Unless otherwise stated, Bible quotations are from the TNIV.

1–7 June

1 Discipleship: following Jesus

Matthew 4:17–25

Disciples were a common feature of the first-century world, both in its Jewish setting as well as its Greek and Roman contexts. The gospels tell us that John the Baptist had disciples, as did the Pharisees. So Jesus, in calling disciples, used a well-known social and educative relationship to further his kingdom.

By shaping his work at this point in the way he does, Matthew emphasises several important things. First, Jesus called his first disciples at the very beginning of his own ministry, when he began to preach repentance and the nearness of the kingdom. Second, Matthew emphasises the efficacy of Jesus' call. His call makes disciples – not human potential or even obedience, but the effective, spoken word of Jesus: '"Come, follow me"… At once they left their nets and followed him' (vv. 19–20). The pattern is repeated for us in the call of James and John, immediately afterwards. Apparently, it was customary for those who would be disciples to ask if they might follow their chosen rabbi; but Jesus, in his humble authority, seeks men (in this case) to follow him, to be his disciples. Third, there is a definite, focused purpose to discipleship, to following Jesus: to 'fish for people' and to make other disciples. Fourth, and most importantly, the call is to follow a person, to be so close to Jesus that they would be 'dusty with the dust of their rabbi', as the saying went. And, fifth, the section that follows verse 23 indicates how these new trainee disciples would learn from Jesus: they would hear his teaching, and they would see his compassion and miraculous power.

It's worth asking ourselves at the outset if our view of discipleship aspires to this biblical model. Most significantly, is our view of discipleship entirely Christ-centred – emphasising his person and his call, his example and his purposes – above the centrality of the church or the individual? What would this look like today?

2   Discipleship: taking up the cross

Matthew 16:21–28

Dietrich Bonhoeffer once said, rather bluntly, that when Christ calls a person, he bids them to come and die. In this, he was seeking to reproduce the full force of Jesus' words about taking up a cross and following him. A true disciple of Jesus, obeying his instruction, will be willing to 'deny themselves and take up their cross and follow' Jesus. It's likely that these three phrases are roughly synonymous, with an emphasis on the last, following Jesus – indeed, these describe and define a life in the presence of Jesus. Life in service and allegiance to Jesus is a life of transformation away from preoccupation with oneself; it's giving up on our own supposed lordship and submitting to another Lord; it's decentralising our thinking away from our own limited and egocentric sphere to a realisation of someone who deserves such focus.

Taking up our cross is essential to the process of discipleship. We notice that this, in itself, is an image from the world of those first disciples. It would conjure up significant resonances for them. First, taking up a cross would be a public act. Walking through the streets to the place of execution would be something witnessed by those standing along the way. Everyone would see and everyone would know. Second, taking up the cross was an excruciatingly painful and heavy burden. Third, taking up the cross indicates a cruel end in sight – death on the cross. Indeed, the sequence that Jesus outlines for himself earlier in the gospel (his obedient decision, suffering, rejection, death and future glory) might well become the sequence of those who follow him.

The rhetorical questions highlight Jesus' intention: 'What good will it be for you to gain the whole world, yet forfeit your soul? Or what can you give in exchange for your soul?' (v. 26). This Matthean episode encourages us to see that, though becoming a disciple is one thing, the seemingly counterintuitive continuation in that faithful adherence – against what appear enormous odds or inconceivable events (see Peter's objection here) – is quite another. To be devoted to Jesus is to put him first, to really prioritise him above everything else that competes for that status – this is how we become worthy of him.

3 Discipleship: loss and inestimable gain

Philippians 3:1–12

Ask the apostle Paul what in life he was pursuing most, and he would no doubt have answered, 'I want to know Christ!' (v. 10). That appears to have been his passionate longing. He elucidates this in the following phrases: 'to know the power of his resurrection and participation in his sufferings'. That's his goal as a disciple of Jesus Christ. And his motivation is simply that there is nothing in life more worthy of his interest than 'the surpassing worth of knowing Christ Jesus my Lord' (v. 8). Later he speaks of his desire to 'gain Christ' (v. 8) and to 'be found in him' (v. 9), and earlier he speaks of boasting in Jesus (v. 3).

He's clear, too, about how he's going to do this. Notice, he says, there is loss involved. Listing aspects of his inheritance and life as a Jew – not all inherently negative – he claims that he intentionally 'considers' them loss (or garbage, dung, rubbish – depending on the translation; v. 7). He *considers* them loss. It's a deliberate action, something he emphasises through repetition. Compared with knowing Christ, everything else is to be judged loss, to be disregarded. There is a faithful determination on the part of Paul. Karl Barth helpfully points out that Paul isn't simply saying that Jesus now comes top of his list, so that he can go back to these things later. The list is gone; knowing Jesus is all.

If there is loss, then there is inestimable gain in knowing Christ, too – gain that surpasses everything else. In knowing Christ, his life is transformed, refashioned and re-forged after the image of the suffering Saviour. He wants to know Christ's resurrection power in order, through the Holy Spirit, to become 'like him in his death' (v. 10). The apostle longs for a cruciform life – a life modelled on Jesus' death: humble, God-pleasing, God-honouring, in service of others, intentional.

Again, we find a few significant aspects of discipleship. First, it centres on the person of Jesus Christ and our ongoing, transforming relationship with him. At its heart, discipleship is about knowing Christ. Second, discipleship is about putting our deepest confidence in Christ and not in anything else. That's an initiative we need to continually take. Third, discipleship, for Paul, is about being conformed to Christ's death in this life – to sacrifice ourselves in service to others, in the name of Christ; to remain committed to Christ crucified in the midst of a suffering world.

4 Discipleship: the centrality of love

John 13:1–5, 34–35

The essential, foundational sign among disciples of Jesus is that we love one another. Indeed, Jesus commands it; it is obligatory for anyone who follows Christ. Jesus speaks of it as a new commandment, not in its insistence – which has Old Testament precedents – but in the standard which is set. We are to love each other as Jesus loved us. This both defines the Christian community and reveals something of God to those as yet without faith. They'll know something of Jesus by witnessing our mutual love together.

How has Jesus loved? John is clear about several aspects of Christ's love. First, Jesus loved his own 'to the end' (v. 1): perfectly, completely, to the full extent. Over three difficult and exacting years of ministry together, Jesus had shown a remarkable depth of love to his disciples, and he'd done this from the initial call that changed everything for them to the very end, the conclusion of their time together. Second, Jesus had loved his disciples even in the midst of antagonism, betrayal, disappointment and satanic activity – Judas sits at the table with the other men even as Jesus serves them. Third, Jesus showed his love by the self-effacing, menial task of washing his disciples' dirty feet – a shameful act, virtually synonymous with slavery. This humble conduct symbolises spiritual washing, but also dramatically prefigures the passion ('lay aside'/'take up') in which Christ's eternal love is shown most graphically.

What magnifies Jesus' humility in this episode is the fact that he was most conscious of his power and status, and that he'd 'come from God and was returning to God' (v. 3), when he rose from the table and served his disciples. Aware of his own glory, his origin and his destiny, he clothed himself in humility and devoted service.

This, then, is the norm, the template, that should direct our discipleship. We must love each other in the same way as Christ loves us: self-sacrificially, humbly, devotedly, perfectly, without regard to our rights or the context we inhabit. As disciples, our lives of Christlike love are to reflect his cruciform example.

5 Discipleship: the significance of community

Matthew 28:16–20

In an individualistic age such as ours, it's good to be reminded that we live out our discipleship in community, not alone – this is one of the significant resources we have in Christ. The resurrected Jesus speaks to the group of worshipping yet doubting disciples (eleven, now that Judas has left them) and commissions them to go and make disciples of others throughout the world, others who will join them and swell the number of disciples forming the nascent church. Followers of Jesus are called upon to encourage others to follow him.

There are four commands that pivot around the idea of making disciples, stressing its central importance: disciples are told to go, to make disciples, to baptise and to teach. Whatever our understanding of baptism, its significance is that through it we enter the people of God, the community, the family of Christ's disciples. This throws up the seeming paradox that discipleship is both an individual and a communal undertaking. It happens within the community to which we now belong. Each of these terms (going, making disciples, baptising, teaching) are 'slow words', as one commentator calls them. They take time. They are not to be rushed. And throughout the whole process, Jesus assures us that he is with us, with universal authority. He himself draws the connection with the word 'therefore' (v. 19).

The church has generally moved from a model of discipleship in which belief is of paramount importance to a more Christlike model in which people are drawn to follow Jesus himself, to belong to a community of Christ-followers and, in that belonging, to learn the Christian faith and to be transformed by it. Jesus doesn't call us or the church to convert others – that's the divine initiative. We're called to witness to the reality of Jesus to a struggling world. We do that, says Christ, in and through community.

6 Discipleship: friendship with Jesus

John 15:9–17

Towards the end of his earthly ministry, Jesus refocuses the disciples' perception of their relationship with him as his disciples. Jesus declares them friends, not merely servants; that is, servants who are also his friends. He does this purely on the grounds that he has revealed to them what the Father had revealed to him: his purpose, his mission. Servants 'do not know their master's business' (v. 15), but nothing is withheld from friends, nothing is concealed; they now have some understanding. As their teacher, Jesus has disclosed the Father's will and demonstrated his love for them. The depth of that love will be clearly seen when he gives his life for them – there is no greater love.

In this new intimacy of understanding, the disciples are called upon to be obedient to Jesus' command that they love one another as he's loved them. Somehow, their love for each other is to reflect that love between the Father and the Son, a love revealed in Christ's love for them: sacrificial, devoted and full of joy.

Finally, we notice that Jesus states that he chose the disciples, his friends, not the other way around. Election is always God's prerogative, as is calling and choice. In a similar way to Israel's election to be witnesses of the fact of the divine presence to those around them, so the disciples' calling and appointment is to 'go and bear fruit' (v. 16). If we ask in Jesus' name for that missional fruit, then the Father will give what we ask – that's Jesus' promise to his friends.

Does it make a difference to our view of discipleship when we define it as friendship with Jesus? It might help us to have a more nuanced idea of being a servant of Christ, of our obedience to him and of our calling. The foundation beneath these complex notions is that Jesus loves us as his chosen friends – loves us enough to lay down his life for us.

Guidelines

Among other things, we have underlined these key areas.

- However we define 'discipleship', it would be good to keep Jesus Christ as central to our understanding and practice. As we've repeatedly observed, this has enormous consequences for discipleship with its implications of devotion, understanding, spiritual life and disciplines, and its outworking in terms of peace, love, healing, proclamation of the good news, reconciliation and renewal.

- We've seen, too, the significance of love in our understanding of discipleship: love for God and for Jesus himself and love for others. Love implies outworking of relationship, so discipleship has not simply to do with internal disciplines of prayer, fasting and the like. We are to go and make disciples, as Jesus did before us.

- Discipleship is to be practised in community, and this has implications for today's church and Christian practice. Those ready to disciple ought to be willing and able to help others feel welcome in the community. Transparent inclusivity is the urgent call for a church wishing to disciple people today.

Having used these brief notes on discipleship this past week, you might like prayerfully to reflect on them within the context of your own life and Christian community.

FURTHER READING
Dietrich Bonhoeffer, *The Cost of Discipleship* (SCM, 2011).
Peter Morden, *The Message of Discipleship* (Inter-Varsity Press, 2018).
Simon Reed, *Followers of the Way: Ancient discipleship for modern Christians* (BRF, 2017).

Matthew 8—10

Andy Angel

Matthew has introduced us to Jesus as the Messiah, son of David and Son of God. He has shown us, through the story of Jesus' birth and early life, that Jesus brings about the fulfilment of God's plan for the covenant people. John the Baptist has proclaimed the coming judgement of God and Jesus has taken up his baton. We have glimpsed his ministry of healing and exorcism, and Jesus has delivered his first block of teaching in the sermon on the mount. The crowds are amazed at his teaching.

Now, Matthew takes us into a series of stories about healing, faith and discipleship. He focuses in on various incidents in Jesus' ministry where he touched the lives of individuals. This is important. Jesus does heal the crowds and delivers them from demon-possession, but his ministry is not presented as one about numbers; it is about God touching the lives of individual people. And he touches the lives of all sorts of people: a leper, a centurion's slave, a disciple's mother-in-law, two violent demoniacs, a paralytic, the daughter of a local leader, a woman with a haemorrhage, two blind men and a deaf mute. Among these, there are people who are socially acceptable, others ostracised from society, some ritually unclean – but all in need of God. Jesus heals them all.

Jesus then trains his disciples for this same mission. He sends them out to proclaim that the kingdom of heaven has drawn near, to heal the sick and to cast out demons. His instructions for mission are deeply challenging. Much as they are given to his disciples for a mission which was specific to first-century Palestine, they remind each of us of the demanding calling we have in following Christ.

Unless otherwise stated, Bible quotations are my own translation.

1 Cleansing the leper

Matthew 8:1–4

This story is deceptively simple and it is easy to miss what is going on in it. First, the word 'leper' here refers to someone with a contagious skin disease. Interestingly, this leper does not ask to be healed but made clean. If someone contracted a skin disease, they had to be examined by a priest. If the disease had taken hold, the leper was pronounced unclean (see Leviticus 13—14). Anyone pronounced unclean was to wear torn clothes, have dishevelled hair and cry out, 'Unclean! Unclean!' They were to live alone outside town until the disease left them (Leviticus 13:45–46). This leper was suffering not only illness but also social isolation. The fact that the leper asks to be made clean shows that he did not just want healing; he also wanted to be pronounced clean and get back to living in community.

The only person who could make a leper clean was a priest, as specified in Leviticus. This leper sees something in Jesus. His opening line, 'If you want to, you can make me clean', suggests faith not simply that Jesus can heal him, but that Jesus can act as a priest, pronouncing him clean and restoring him to society. Jesus' response, 'I do want to, be cleansed', shows that he knows he has a priestly as well as a healing ministry.

Jesus the priest later pronounces destruction on the temple (24:1–4). But he does not wade in immediately to replace the old order. While the temple stands, Jesus respects the commands of the law. In line with the regulations in Leviticus 13—14, Jesus commands the man to show himself to the priest and make the appropriate offering. His words 'as a witness to them' most likely suggest that Jesus wants the priests to know he follows the law. For those of us with a gung-ho attitude towards the law, the priesthood and the temple, this story ought to make us stop and think. Although he knows God will judge the temple and priesthood, Jesus acts with humility and respect towards them until that day.

2 A centurion and his *pais*

Currently, this story appears in discussions around homosexuality. Luke tells a similar story in which a centurion has a slave (Greek: *doulos*) who is desperately ill (Luke 7:1-10). Matthew says that the centurion has a *pais* who is suffering terribly. The Greek *pais* can mean son or slave. Do Matthew and Luke record two different incidents, where one centurion has a son and the other a slave? Or do they record the same event? If so, was it a son or a slave? Or does *pais* mean slave in Matthew? And some are asking: if so, is this the kind of slave with whom the centurion might have had a sexual relationship? After all, *pais* has the same word stem as *paiderastia*, which was the form of Greek love where a young man had a sexual relationship with a younger man or boy.

There is nothing in the story that suggests such a relationship between the centurion and his *pais*. The word *pais* can mean son or slave without a hint of sexual relationship. The Lukan story says the slave is highly prized (Luke 7:2) but that does not require sexual interpretation. So this line of hermeneutic has no support from the text itself. And if it did, it would land biblical Christians in a quandary, as a *pais* is normally a prepubescent boy – and that would have Jesus seemingly colluding with a child molester. But given the lack of evidence for this interpretation, we need not be concerned.

Nevertheless, this is a highly controversial story. Jesus tells members of the covenant people, who are oppressed by Roman rule, that they lack faith in comparison with this centurion. Not only that, but that sons of the kingdom (i.e. members of the covenant people) would not enjoy the feasting in the new Jerusalem while others from outside Judea (i.e. most likely Gentiles) would. This turns hope on its head and seems to reward sinners. But Jesus' words get right to the heart of sin and righteousness. The centurion has faith *in Jesus*. God calls people into covenant relationship with him through faith in Jesus. A question we should always be asking ourselves is whether we are living according to our own construction of Jesus, or according to his words and actions in the gospels, which tell us who he truly is.

3 Healing the mother-in-law

What I am about to say I have written before, but it bears repeating in a world where we rightly worry about the marginalisation of people created equally in the image of God. Peter's mother-in-law is something of a gospel heroine. She remains unnamed, which might worry us that Matthew as author marginalises her. But this is not true. She is healed and immediately gets up to serve. She gets what Jesus is about; her famous son-in-law does not. Jesus calls Peter 'Satan' because he does not understand that the Son of Man came to serve (20:24–28) and calls others to serve (16:21–28). By contrast, she gets it. Jesus heals her and she serves him. She is an example to us all.

In fact, she is not so anonymous. Her story is told; many other healing stories are not. Jesus healed many people and cast out demons from many others. People were bringing the demon-possessed and those who were ill to him seemingly constantly. Their stories are all lumped together into summary accounts like this one (for another, see 4:23–25). There were too many healings to record them all. Peter's mother-in-law has her story told, so that we can hear it and follow her example. Sometimes, as readers of the text with our own concerns, we need to be careful not to allow our issues to dominate our reading so fully that we fail to see what the text is doing.

But for Matthew, all these stories point to who Jesus is (v. 17). These healings demonstrate that Jesus is the one who fulfils the words of the prophet: 'He himself has taken our weaknesses, and has carried our diseases' (Isaiah 53:4). We tend to assume that Isaiah 53 is about vicarious suffering for our sins, but this is not what Matthew draws out of it. Matthew applies the text to Jesus' ministry of healing physically and spiritually, which figures large in his portrait of Jesus. Although during the Reformation, many Protestant churches lost this aspect of the ministry of the risen Christ among us, it has thankfully re-entered the Protestant bloodstream. Given that Jesus heals too many to mention in the gospels, we ought to expect this to be part of his ministry among us today.

4 Following Jesus

I have heard these stories interpreted in ways that suggest Jesus was speaking to people with little to no faith. This is not so. The scribe hears Jesus give the order to go over to the other side of the lake and thinks it applies to him. He tells Jesus that he will go wherever Jesus goes. He shows real commitment. Matthew introduces the other person as 'another one of Jesus' disciples'. Matthew clearly believes that the scribe and this other man (the Greek indicates this unnamed disciple is male) are not only part of the crowd following Jesus but disciples. We hear the significance of Jesus' responses to them both more accurately when we recognise this.

Jesus challenges the first on the basis of his own words. He hears Jesus' order to move and tells him he will go wherever Jesus does. So, Jesus responds by telling him what this entails. He is an itinerant preacher. He moves about and does not have a home. Note that Jesus does not discourage him. He simply tells this scribe disciple what following him means. We ought to take time to listen to what we say to Jesus and listen for his response. I once knew a church organist who refused to play 'All to Jesus I Surrender', as she could not lead the congregation in a hymn that she knew we did not mean. I think she had got the measure of the way Jesus hears our words.

The challenge to the other disciple needs a little unpacking. His request was to be able to stay at home until his father died, so that he could bury him properly. Understood in the culture of the ancient Near East, this is what his words mean. Jesus responds that he should follow him now. Those who do not have enough spiritual life in them can wait around to fulfil this family duty. Jesus' reply does not mean he could not go back to bury his father when he did die, nor does it mean that this father's corpse should be left to lie unburied. However, the challenge remains stark: follow me in preference to your perceived family duties. These days, when many put rest, children's sports, family time and the beach on a sunny day before weekly worship, for example, these words of Jesus regain life and challenge.

5 Stilling a storm

This is the first of two sea miracle stories. This one poses a question: 'What kind of person is this, because the winds and the waves obey him?' The other one (14:22–33) answers it. Both stories give all the clues necessary to finding the answer by using an ancient Jewish myth. This myth pictures God as coming to earth on a cloud chariot to rescue his people (or a righteous person) from being engulfed in the mythical waters of chaos or from being destroyed by the dragon (Leviathan or Rahab) that lives within these waters. God dries up the sea or splits it in two where it does not flee from his presence. He kills the dragon. We find this myth in Psalms 18, 74, 77 and 89, for example. We find fragments of it in parts of Job (e.g. 3:3–11; 9:2–14; 26:2–14) and various prophets (e.g. Habakkuk 3). We are probably all familiar with it from the book of Revelation. Quite often, God rebukes the sea and it dries up or flees (e.g. Psalm 18:15).

Matthew paints the picture of the disciples in the boat with the colour palette of this myth. Literally, he says there was a great earthquake in the sea and the boat was being flooded by waves; those following God are being engulfed in the sea. The disciples certainly think they will die. Jesus rebukes the wind and the sea, and they calm down. Jesus takes on the role of God rebuking the chaos sea and dragon. Matthew drops a hint as to the answer to the question the disciples later ask.

But this is no lesson in cognitively taking on board facts about Jesus. This is a story about whole-life discipleship. The disciples are not watching this take place from the safety of the shore so that they can know that Jesus is the God who conquers chaos and evil. They are in the boat so that they can understand that God conquers chaos and experience what it means. Jesus sometimes takes us to places that are distinctly uncomfortable, and there he seeks to grow our little faith. When, in those situations, we wonder exactly what kind of a person he is, we find ourselves in good company.

6 Demoniacs in Gadara

Matthew 8:28—9:1

There was a flourishing literature in the first century which told of battles of armies of demons fighting the angelic armies of God. It finds its roots in the myth of God battling the dragon and the sea. In some texts, the enemies of God are cast into the sea or the abyss when God wins the victory over them. There are clearly overtones of this in the story here.

The two demoniacs cry out, 'What have you to do with us?', a question only ever addressed in the Old Testament and Apocrypha to enemies (Judges 11:12; 2 Kings 3:13; 2 Chronicles 35:21; 2 Esdras 1:24). The demons know Jesus is their enemy. They know God will win in the end and they will be punished in eternal torment. So they ask if Jesus has come to torment them before this time. They name Jesus 'Son of God', because in ancient Jewish exorcism, using a spirit's name gave you authority over them. They try to overpower Jesus. However, they know what is coming, so they ask to go into the pigs. They run headlong into the sea – just as demons are cast into the abyss at the end of time.

But there is a human story here, too. Two men are demon-possessed. They are so out of control that others stay away from where they live. They live around tombs, with the dead rather than the living. The demons control their actions as they approach Jesus. However, they are delivered from these demons. But there is tragedy in the human story, too. The herdsmen go off and tell the locals what has happened to the two demon-possessed men. Matthew uses a Greek present participle for 'demon-possessed' here, rather than a past participle, which would be more accurate, as they are no longer possessed. It appears that in the minds of the locals, they are still demoniacs. The townsfolk are also more concerned about the pigs. Rather than asking Jesus to stay because of his delivering members of their community from demon-possession, they ask him to leave because of the loss of the pigs and income. Sometimes, the work of God is disruptive. Are we the kind of people who welcome it in all its messiness or shun it?

Guidelines

There is a lot about the nature of faith in the stories this week. Although Jesus has been healing and restoring lives, he has also been challenging people with the nature of faith. Sometimes the work of God disrupts our patterns of life, and we need to count the cost. We need to be prepared for things to change as God does something new, in us and around us. God may take us to places we might rather not go and into situations which may seem more chaotic than we would like. He calls us to trust in him in those situations until the moment when things calm down again. He challenges us in our commitment. When we say we have committed to live entirely for him, he shows us areas of life where we might rather not let go of what we have and do. He calls us to greater commitment, and that can involve making sacrifices. He does heal and restore us, but as he does so he calls us to serve. As children of Abraham, we are called not simply to be blessed but also to be a blessing to the nations (Genesis 12:1–3). And above all, he calls us to have faith in him.

There is much to think through here for each of us. Where are we in our own faith journey? It can be very easy to settle down by the roadside. When we have learned the ropes of basic Christian spirituality, we can settle all too easily for a pattern of life which stays the same and may be good, but is not all we are called to do or to be. When we have got the basics of Christian teaching under our belts, it can be easy to rest in the knowledge that we know what it is all about, and we can settle for far less of a knowledge of and relationship with Christ than he calls us to. Sitting down by the roadside can also lead us into accepting the way things are, when God might want change. Let's not settle for anything less than what the Lord calls us into each day, and let's make it our daily prayer to ask him who he would have us be and what he would have us do.

1 Healing a paralytic

Here, once again, Jesus seems to have a different agenda. What impressed him about the centurion was his faith, and this is what Jesus drew attention to, rather than his healing of the boy or slave. In this story, the people who bring the paralytic to Jesus on his bed are clearly looking for a miracle of healing. When Jesus sees their faith in him, he comments on it.

Just as his delight in the faith of the centurion led him to talk about who would enjoy the delights of feasting in the kingdom of heaven, here his pleasure at their faith leads him to forgive the sins of the paralytic. Jesus' focus seems to be on the glorious kingdom which is to come, and the forgiveness of sins which is so necessary for any who would enter the kingdom on the day God comes to judge.

Some of the scribes worry inwardly that this man does not have authority to forgive sins. Jesus heals the paralytic to demonstrate to them that he does have this authority. Interestingly, he refers to himself as the Son of Man with regard to his authority to forgive sins. While the debate about this title or description still rages, in Matthew the Son of Man is the one who comes to judge at the end of time (e.g. 25:31). So Jesus claims that he, the one who will come at the end of time to judge all, is also the one who has authority to forgive sins in advance of that day.

The man is healed of his paralysis. His friends carried him on his bed to Jesus, but he walks home carrying his bed himself. Although the text is silent here, it is hard to imagine that the man's friends were anything but ecstatic about his healing. But for Jesus and Matthew, this miracle is a sign. It points to the greater miracle of forgiveness of sins and entrance into the kingdom of heaven when Jesus comes again. This story is timeless. In a church culture where healing has once again been embraced by many, we can tend to focus on miracles in this life above the true miracle of life in the next. Many of us would do well to look at the miraculous with Jesus' eyes.

2 Tax collectors and sinners

Matthew 9:9–13

Equally timeless is this story of Jesus' rebuke of the Pharisees. It probably helps to put it into historical context. The Pharisees shared with Jesus a love for the commands of God. They shared with Jesus a hope for the coming of God's kingdom. Jesus even told his disciples to listen to the Pharisees (23:2–3). However, they disagreed on some things. The Pharisees added to the commands of God in order to keep people from breaking them. Before contemporary Christians point a finger, we ought to consider how frequently, in our spirituality and literature, we add to the commands of Jesus. One of their additions to the law of God was holiness in table fellowship – which meant not eating with sinners.

Hence, they are quite shocked when Jesus eats with Matthew and his tax-collector friends and associates and with assorted other sinners. Jesus breaks no law in doing this. To be fair, the Pharisees do not accuse him of breaking any command, either. They are just a bit surprised that his spiritual practice does not involve holiness in table fellowship. They do not seem to make that much of a fuss either. They ask Jesus' disciples what is going on rather than publicly challenging Jesus.

On the contrary, it is Jesus who challenges them. He overhears them talking to his disciples and challenges their spirituality and table fellowship customs. They try to bring the holiness of the temple into daily life to honour God, and Jesus challenges this with a quotation of Hosea 6:6. God desires mercy rather than temple sacrifices. So Jesus' spirituality is about showing mercy to others rather than bringing holiness appropriate only to the temple into daily life.

His saying, 'I have not come to call the righteous but sinners', trips all too easily off our tongues. I don't think I have ever belonged to a Christian group which did not feel uncomfortable when God answered our prayers for growth by bringing disruptive and disturbed people into our fellowship. I have belonged to far too many such groups where Christians seem much keener to evangelise socially easy and basically sorted people. Quite often, our outreach programmes are much better suited to bringing such people into church. Next time God brings a thief, vandal, adulterer or really needy person whose life is a complete mess into your church, praise God for his mercy and live it out.

3 The bridegroom

Matthew 9:14–17

The disciples of John the Baptist are rather bolder than the Pharisees, in that they do approach Jesus directly, asking why they and the Pharisees fast but not the disciples of Jesus. The disciples of John and the Pharisees were preparing for the coming kingdom. They hoped that God would come and rescue his people. Within Jewish tradition, fasting seems to have been a practice which was undertaken as a prayer to hasten the day God would act to save his people (among other things). So Isaiah 58:3 has the covenant people moaning that they fast and God does not rescue them. God replies that their fast is not the kind of fast he looks for in the covenant people. The kingdom had not yet come, so it made perfect sense for the Pharisees and disciples of John to fast.

Jesus replies with this saying about the bridegroom. Bridegroom imagery could refer to more than one thing in contemporary Judaism. It was related to the coming of the Messiah in John 2:4. Isaiah 62:5 compares God's rescuing the covenant people and rebuilding Zion to the rejoicing of a bridegroom over his bride. So when Jesus compares himself to a bridegroom here, he indicates that the Messiah is present or that in his ministry God has come to rescue his people. Therefore, it is not appropriate for his followers to fast. Time with the bridegroom is time for partying.

This makes for interesting reading when brought alongside Jesus' teaching on fasting in 6:16–18, not least as he begins, 'whenever you fast', not 'when you used to fast'. Perhaps, we can soften the disjunction between these sayings if we focus on the other half of Jesus' reply in verse 15. The day will come when Jesus will be taken away from his disciples and this will be a day for fasting. We get the same idea of Jesus being absent as bridegroom in the parable in 25:1–13. But although he may be absent in the sense that he has not yet brought in the kingdom of heaven, he remains present daily with his disciples as our teacher until the day he comes again as Son of Man (28:19–20) – and as our teacher, he prepares us for the coming of his kingdom.

4 Raising a girl and healing a woman

Matthew 9:18–26

As a parish priest, I take funerals. They are occasions of mixed emotions and reactions: grief, joy, nostalgia, despair, regret and gratitude, to name a few. The shock of loss often creates confusion. Appropriate pastoral care is so important, not least in funeral services. The families in this story are going through this process. The ruler knows his daughter has died and comes to Jesus to bring her back to life. Today, we would say he was in denial – understandable when his daughter was so very young. While this ruler seeks Jesus to bring her back from the dead, the family are clearly arranging appropriate mourning. It was traditional to hire clarinet players for mourning ceremonies (e.g. 'Rabbi Judah says: even the poorest in Israel should not hire less than two clarinets and one wailing woman', Mishnah, tractate Ketubbot 4:4). By the time Jesus gets to the house, the clarinet players are already leading the mourning. It is hard not to wonder whether others in the family want to get on with grieving while this father is fighting reality, hard not to wonder what tensions are in the air.

I used to train priests in a theological college, and I now train lay and ordained ministers in a parish context. What Jesus does here is striking – not least because you would never encourage (or permit) a minister in training to go anywhere near following his example. First, he stops on the way to the ruler's house to attend to somebody else. Then he uses seemingly insensitive language – why call this woman 'daughter' when the ruler is present, his daughter dead, and waiting for Jesus to come to his home? Then he tells everybody the girl is not dead when everybody knows she is. You cannot help wondering whether the laughter was in complete disbelief.

Yet, the father is right: Jesus does have the power to bring his little girl back from the dead. Jesus stretches out his hand and she is raised. No wonder the news spread. Sometimes, we forget that we have put Jesus in a box of our making. He can do more than we expect or imagine. Perhaps, like this father, we ought to take the risk of believing him more often.

5 Two blind men

Matthew 9:27–31

The story is as old as the gospel: people seek healing and are amazed by it, but healing does not necessarily produce faith – let alone faithfulness. We do not know what the woman healed of the haemorrhage or the ruler did after Jesus left, but both those stories give a positive assessment of their faith. This next healing story does not end on such a positive note.

The blind men have faith. They are following Jesus. Matthew uses the same word as he does of disciples following Jesus faithfully (Greek: *akolutheō*). They even follow him into the house where he is going. They are calling out to him to have mercy on them. They call him 'Son of David'. This seems to reflect their desire for healing, as there was a Jewish tradition that Solomon was an exorcist and healer. When asked, they claim that they really do believe that Jesus can heal them. They clearly do have this faith as Jesus says, 'Let it happen to you according to your faith', and then their eyes are opened. However, their faith in Jesus seems to be limited to what they can receive. It does not stretch as far as obedience. Jesus gives them one instruction and they go away and immediately disobey. He commands that they tell absolutely nobody, and they go out and tell people throughout the whole area what he has done. It does not really matter what his reason for giving this instruction was (and many suggestions have been made). The point is that he gave them an instruction and they did not follow it.

Jesus' words towards the end of the sermon on the mount seem to echo through the air. He spoke of many calling out to him 'Lord, Lord' on the day he comes again about their amazing ministries of power, healing and exorcism but his turning them away because they were not obedient (7:21–23). These two blind men are the recipients of healing rather than those exercising the ministry of healing. However, their focus seems to be on the miracle of healing rather than obedience to Jesus. This story and Jesus' words make it clear which Jesus values more.

6 Healing a deaf mute

Matthew 9:32–34

Now people bring to Jesus a man who is *kōphos*. This word can mean deaf or mute. Given that on being healed he speaks, this man is probably mute. He is also probably deaf, because this is the only story of a *kōphos* hearing before Jesus claims in 11:5 that the deaf (Greek: *kōphoi*) hear as a result of his ministry. This story concerns the healing of a deaf mute.

This man was also demon-possessed. When the demon was cast out, he spoke. Illness and demon-possession are linked elsewhere in Matthew (e.g. 17:14–18). However, illness and demon-possession are not always linked. No demons were cast from the two blind men or the woman with the haemorrhage. Nor were any demons cast out of the little girl who had died. Demon-possession and illness are sometimes distinguished; for example, 8:16 has Jesus healing the sick and casting out demons from the possessed as two separate activities. Stories like the present one cannot be used to suggest that illness is caused by demon-possession (as has sometimes been done). Reading the story within the gospel healing and exorcism tradition as a whole does not support this idea.

Reactions to Jesus are quite stark. Some are amazed and impressed. They claim that nothing like this has ever been seen in Israel. This is not entirely true – not least if we understand Israel to be the people rather than the land. Elijah and Elisha performed many similar miracles. If we include the partings of the Red Sea and the Jordan and the falling of the walls of Jericho, we have to conclude that these people are exaggerating. On the other side, the Pharisees have moved position from simply questioning why he ate with tax collectors and sinners (9:11). They clearly do not approve of his stance on issues where their traditions and his practice diverge. So although they do not deny the miracles, they read them through their theological lens – Jesus' works must be those of the ruler of demons. Neither reaction is fully appropriate – although one has more faith than the other. This leaves me wondering about my reaction to the past and present healing ministry of Jesus. Is it appropriate?

Guidelines

There have been a lot of healing stories in the last week. There are a lot of healing stories in the gospels, and there are many summary passages which give the reader an idea of Jesus' general ministry before the gospel writer focuses on particular incidents again. These summary passages always mention Jesus' healing and exorcism ministry. The way the gospels present the ministry of Jesus, it seems that healings and exorcisms were a large part of it.

'*Were* a large part of it.' Why not *are*? Within some Christian denominations, prayer for healing and the ministry of exorcism have always been part of the ministry of the churches. Within others, they are deemed no longer to be part of the ministry of the church. I grew up as a Protestant (low-church Anglican) in churches which, by and large, did not practise any kind of healing ministry, except for praying for the sick within the intercessions in Sunday services and at house groups. On preparing for ministry, I studied the healing ministry of the church and discovered to my surprise that Protestants are something of an anomaly here. They rejected the healing ministry (or much of it) at the Reformation as a Catholic practice not to be emulated – despite the clear call to it in the book of James (5:13–18). It was one of those moments when I realised that my Roman Catholic brothers and sisters were much more biblical than I was in this area of ministry.

As contemporary readers of scripture, we can easily fall into reading miracle stories for their meaning. We look beyond the basic text to see what deeper spiritual meaning lies beneath the story. This can be important and sometimes may be exactly what we ought to be doing as readers. There is a long history within the church of looking for such meaning in the text. But there is also a long tradition of healing ministry within the church, which is rooted in the ministry of Jesus about which we have been reading this week. It is important to recognise that these stories are first and foremost stories of healing, bearing witness to this important aspect of the ministry of Christ, both then and now.

1 Prayer and mission

Matthew 9:35—10:4

Jesus continues with what can only be described as a busy ministry. Note the detail: 'healing every disease and every sickness' (v. 35) – 'every'. He went around all the towns and all the villages – 'all'. He must have encountered a lot of people. Matthew suggests so. 'Seeing the crowds' – 'crowds' plural. Jesus' reaction is the really interesting detail; he had compassion on them. The word used literally means 'he was gutted' (Greek: *esplangch-nisthē*). As he went around teaching and healing, what he saw of people's need for wholeness and holiness moved him profoundly.

Wholeness and holiness. Jesus was not simply concerned with healing people and casting out demons, though he did both these things. He clearly wanted to bring people physical health and spiritual freedom. However, he also went around teaching: he went to their synagogues; he taught people how to live in obedience to God's commands. That is what rabbis did, and that is what Jesus did in the sermon on the mount. He wanted to enable people to live in holiness.

He knows he needs a team to share the burden of the work. He sees the number of people who just look lost; they are helpless and hassled and do not seem to be getting very far in their search for wholeness and holiness. So Jesus tells his disciples what the problem is, what the challenge is, and instructs them to pray about it. Because a new chapter begins at this point, we can stop here and fail to read to the end of the story. Having asked all his disciples to pray, Jesus calls the twelve and he gives them authority over unclean spirits and to heal every disease and illness. He gives them the power to continue his ministry of healing and exorcism. They become the answer to their prayer.

Or part of the answer. Jesus does not yet commission them to teach. He has more to teach them and they will not be able to take part in this aspect of his ministry until he has done so. That commission comes in the final verses of this gospel. Jesus calls and equips, but he does not call until he knows that we are ready and able.

2 A very specific mission

Matthew 10:5-15
Jesus' mission instructions to his disciples here are very specific. Do not go to the Gentiles (Greek: *ethne*) and do not go to the Samaritans. Only go to the lost sheep of the house of Israel. These directives are very different from those at the end of the gospel. In his final instructions (28:18-20), Jesus commands his disciples to go and make disciples of all the nations or Gentiles (Greek: *ethne*). There is no point trying to twist the text to make these the same mission. They are clearly different.

Interestingly, a similar pattern emerges in Jesus' teaching about the end times. The Son of Man comes to all the tribes of the land (Greek: *pasai hai phulai tēs gēs*, quoting Zechariah 12:10, which refers to the tribes of Israel) in 24:29-35. When the Son of Man takes his throne of judgement in 25:31-32, all the Gentiles or nations (Greek: *panta ta ethne*) gather before him. Matthew has a pattern of mission and judgement first to the Jews and then the Gentiles. It does not seem so far away from Paul, who sees judgement and glory coming first for the Jew and then for the Greek (Romans 2:9-10). So this mission is not the same as the great commission in Matthew 28.

In that sense, we are not bound by these mission instructions, as this is not the mission with which we are entrusted. That is the mission in the great commission, at the end of the gospel. This mission was for Jesus' disciples in the first century – as we shall see further as we work through Jesus' instructions and predictions in this mission discourse. Even so, it is the same Jesus who sends us and so we can expect him to send us in similar ways. We can expect his missional calling to come at a cost; we can expect him to send us to specific peoples or communities; we can expect him to call us to something we find challenging. The question is, will we respond as these first disciples did – in obedience?

3 Prudence and purity

We have today one of the most misrepresented sayings of Jesus, where he calls us to be as prudent as serpents and as unsophisticated as doves. Perhaps not everybody's experience is the same as mine, but I suspect many have heard this verse used to justify forms of behaviour which are not readily recognisable as lovingly Christian: from being disingenuous, guarded and canny to playing politics in a less-than-friendly manner. It is as if we follow the command to love our neighbour up to the point where we think that we now need to invoke Jesus' instruction to take the gloves off. This does no justice to Jesus' words.

Jesus commands the twelve to be prudent. He instructs them to have practical wisdom, to do things which make sense in the difficult situations they will encounter. He tells them to be sensible. Too often we read the command in the light of our estimation of serpents and think Jesus has given us permission to be wily and dishonest. Not so. Jesus makes this perfectly clear in his instruction that we are to be as pure or unsophisticated as doves. The term he uses literally means 'unmixed'. This is a far cry from the duplicitousness which some have used this saying to justify.

The context of this instruction is the mission of the twelve to Israel which took place in the first century. Jesus says in verse 23 that the Son of Man would come in judgement before they had completed the task. This happened in AD70, when the Romans took Jerusalem as they put down a Jewish revolt which had begun around AD66. (There is huge controversy surrounding Jesus' Son of Man sayings, to which I cannot do justice in a short reflection, but see the further reading.) This instruction is not even directed to us in our mission to the Gentiles today. So if we are to apply it to our own situations, we ought to do so with the prudence and purity to which Jesus called the twelve. We are to act transparently and with integrity as we stay true to all Jesus' commands in all the tricky situations we face.

4 Boldness

In yesterday's reading, Jesus made it quite clear to his disciples that they would suffer physical beatings and trials for calling Israel to repentance. The early chapters of the book of Acts offer us a window into the persecution that these early Christians suffered in Palestine. Now Jesus tells the disciples not to expect to be treated any differently from the way people treated him. As his followers, the twelve could expect the people in Palestine to whom they were offering the hope of the gospel to treat them as children of Satan – after all, they identified Jesus with Beelzebub, the prince of demons (9:34). This is remarkably stark. I cannot remember hearing in any Christian mission training event words to the effect that we might be identified as children of Satan, just like Jesus was.

In the face of such suffering, Jesus instructs the twelve to remain bold. What Jesus has taught them secretly, as he took them aside to explain what he had been preaching to the crowds, they should shout from the rooftops. As they do this, they must not fear any who oppose them. Instead, they must fear the living God, because he is the one who has power to cast body and soul into hell. Jesus encourages them to recognise that they have inestimable value in his sight. Hence, they should own him publicly, so that when he comes in judgement, Jesus does not disown them for their failure to proclaim him and his teaching.

Again, these commands concern a mission which was undertaken in the first century. However, something in Jesus' words here cuts right across our culture. Jesus combines our personal worth in God's sight with his judgement of us. In our practical spirituality today, we more often than not separate the two and prefer self-worth to judgement. In doing so, we are probably imitating the pattern of contemporary secular culture. By contrast, Jesus calls us both to understand that we are invaluable to God and to completely dedicate our lives to him – and to tell others about it.

5 Finding and losing life

Jesus' words to his disciples here are anything but figurative. He knows that his message will cut right through the middle of the religious and political life of his Palestinian Jewish contemporaries. So it was unlikely to be any different for his disciples as they proclaimed the hope of the gospel in the face of God's impending judgement in the form of the destruction of Jerusalem and its temple, which took place in AD70. He reworks a prophecy from Micah 7:6 to acknowledge that even ones nearest and dearest may not be with you as you wait for the salvation of God. He tells the twelve that they must not put any family ties above their commitment to him. In a culture like our own, where family bonds are weakening, this seems harsh enough. In first-century Palestine, where family bonds were strong, this was extremely challenging.

However, Jesus does not stop there. He tells his disciples to be prepared to pay the ultimate cost; they must be willing to lay down their lives for him. To take up one's cross was to carry the instrument of one's execution on one's back to the place of execution. Crucifixion was the most feared death in the ancient Roman world. Jesus' words here would have sent a shudder through his disciples.

After Jesus' own crucifixion, the disciples did not have the power to live them out (or the instruction to continue in mission) until the day of Pentecost. Then the Spirit came. The stories in the early chapters of the book of Acts tell of disciples who were empowered remarkably to live out exactly the mission to which Jesus calls them in these instructions – as they proclaimed the good news of Jesus to those in Palestine, despite, in and through persecutions. Jesus calls all his disciples (not just the twelve in the first century) to take up their crosses and follow him. We cannot do this in our own strength but, as the example of those first disciples testifies, we can in the power of the Spirit. Let us, like them, call on the Spirit to empower us in our witness today.

6 Generous judgement

Whoever makes a cup of tea for the CEO will receive not only their annual wages but their bonus, too. People would be rushing for their kettles. Someone would be paying out a great deal of money to all the tea-makers, and well beyond the normal price for serving tea. Jesus promises similarly generous rewards here. He looks forward to the day of judgement and says that those who have shown hospitality to prophets and righteous people (both types of ministers of Jesus' gospel) will receive the very same rewards as prophets and righteous people. Even someone who simply gives a cup of cold water to one of the disciples whom Jesus sends on this mission will not lose their reward. What if the most notorious sinners gave out the odd cup of cold water to Peter or James? What if they were unrepentant? Jesus' words are quite remarkable. He simply makes an unqualified statement of how God will reward those who are hospitable towards his ministers and disciples. Sounds rather like the generosity shown towards Rahab in Joshua 2 and 6.

This ought to make us stop and pause. Whether we accept the traditional teaching about the resurrection of the dead, the judgement of God and eternal reward or punishment, or we find aspects of these teachings difficult, Jesus' words should stop us in our tracks. Sometimes we can present the subject of the judgement of God in overly simplistic ways. But what Jesus says here defies such simplistic schemas – though without contradicting the rest of what Jesus says in the gospels. It presumes there will be a judgement. It presumes there will be rewards, and there is no indication that Jesus changed his mind about punishments here. It simply states that those who have helped in the mission of God in any way will receive an amazing reward. God wants to save people from judgement and he promises great rewards for those who are in any way involved in this ministry. He loves to save. He loves to bless. He calls his disciples to call others from judgement to salvation and wants to reward *anyone and everyone involved in any way* in bringing people to repentance and faith.

Guidelines

This section of Matthew can be puzzling. The promise of the coming of the Son of Man before the disciples complete the mission to Israel (10:23) can cause problems. The trust demanded of the disciples as they set out in mission with so little can seem to set the bar quite high for anyone thinking about ministry. Jesus' sayings about not being worthy of him if we do not give our all can be frightening. There is much here to worry the sensitive soul. Reading these instructions as applying to the disciples in the first century, and reading the coming of the Son of Man as being about God's judgement on unrepentant Israel in AD70, can soften the shock of the text – because then it no longer applies to us.

But I hope that I have not softened the shock by reading the text this way. Jesus' challenges to his disciples echo his teachings more generally to all his disciples throughout time. His call to discipleship is never less than a call to total giving of ourselves in love and service. There are many things in this passage which could and should shock us into greater commitment, but there is one thought above all others from this section that I would like us to dwell on for a moment.

How important must it be to God, if he makes an unqualified promise of reward to any who help support Christian mission in any way? How much must God long to save people from judgement? What kind of love must burn in the Father's heart, if he lavishes blessing on sinners who show basic acts of generosity to ministers of the gospel? Certainly, a love to save people. Most definitely, a love for mission. Does the same love burn in our hearts? How much do we long to see people come to faith in Jesus Christ? Will we proclaim Christ as he called his first disciples to do? Or, if we find this rather difficult, are we prepared to learn? I hope so – because we simply do not know the love of the Father if we do not engage in mission. The love of God is missional love… but I must stop here, because that is the story of another gospel.

FURTHER READING

Andrew R. Angel, *Chaos and the Son of Man: The Hebrew Chaoskampf tradition in the period 515BCE to 200CE* (Clark, 2006).

R.T. France, *The Gospel of Matthew* (Eerdmans, 2007).

N.T. Wright, *Jesus and the Victory of God* (SPCK, 1996).

Challenges 20:20

David Walker

I suspect that very little of our Christian scriptures, either Old or New Testament, was written in an era of peace and plenty. Rather, in those centuries when writing was produced, copied and conveyed by hand, our biblical books were composed to address the most testing topics of the day. Their authors wrote their words in response to the abiding challenge of how human beings live both individually and as part of society, under God's rule. Yet, while God himself may be unchanging, each age and place presents its own very particular context, which shapes and focuses the human response. For the Old Testament, the particular circumstances might involve corrupt leadership, enemy threats and even exile. The world of the New Testament takes us from Roman occupation and the persecution of the nascent church to the question of how we can withstand the pressures of an alien and morally decadent culture.

The readings and reflections for these next two weeks seek to bring out from the store of scripture passages that explore some of the bigger themes that underlie what it means to live as a Christian, and be part of the Christian church, in the year 2020. Our challenges are no less pressing than those faced by the first readers of our texts. Even while the specifics differ, the broad themes remain constant. We too can feel under threat from a culture changing in ways that push us towards the margins, in a society enthralled by powerful organisations or beset by faltering and fallible leadership.

Our reflections will allow us to draw from the wisdom of the Bible, and its core values and principles – we might even call them 'guidelines' – will help us navigate our challenges.

Unless otherwise stated, Bible quotations are taken from the NRSV.

1 Living in obedience

Romans 13:1–10

The apostle Paul believes in good order. Unlike Peter, who, as recorded in Acts 12, escapes prison by night when his chains are loosened, in Acts 16 Paul remains in his cell until morning. He even insists the authorities bring him out, calling on his rights as a Roman citizen. So, here in his letter to Rome, he advocates obedience to the secular authorities. It's an uncomfortable passage at first sight to readers in the present day, where all manner of authorities are disrespected, assumed to be driven by sinful motives or at least targets for overt challenge and ridicule. Should we really shut up and follow orders? What, then, of those ordered to do grossly wrong things under unjust regimes – should they obey too? And if the authorities are God-given, is it not therefore wrong for Christians to campaign for changes to the laws they have enacted? Perhaps politics and religion really mustn't be mixed.

If we stopped reading Paul's words at verse 7, we might be justified in taking that as his view. But the second half of today's passage puts a very different slant on his meaning, taking us back to the very heart of his theology. Paul echoes the words of both the gospels and the Old Testament in placing love of neighbour at the centre of the law. Human authorities are set in post by God to create and enforce laws and to levy taxes, but the lesser law is always subservient to the greater. Indeed, Paul himself disobeys the authorities who had sent him on his mission to Damascus, deserting his post after he met with Jesus. Where any human authority flies in the face of love, it is open to Christians to disobey, while recognising that the penalty for such disobedience may be exacted upon them.

Moreover, in our present day, our constitutions, written or unwritten, set out that our lawmakers operate only with the consent of the people. We elect representatives and, when dissatisfied with their rule, we replace them with their opponents. In this, we have authority ourselves, an authority that is just as God-given as that which resides in presidents and prime ministers. With our authority comes the responsibility to exercise it wisely, first by using our vote, second by campaigning for better laws and third by acting out or speaking up against injustice. This is what true obedience to the law requires.

2 The welfare of the city

Jeremiah 29:1–14

Jerusalem has fallen and its leaders carted off to Babylon. The vision of an independent kingdom, faithful to God as his chosen people, appears to be over. Jeremiah's warnings have been vindicated and his opponents exposed as frauds. So what is Jeremiah, himself still in Jerusalem, God's special city, to say next?

Jeremiah's letter steers his readers in an unexpected direction. He doesn't direct them to a life of quiet, separatist purity. They are not to keep their heads down and themselves apart from their Gentile conquerors, in the way that many religious minorities cope with their inferior status in an alien society. Nor does Jeremiah advocate active, or even passive, resistance to the forces that have taken them into exile. Instead, they are to 'seek the welfare of the city' where God has sent them. They are to pray for its well-being even while they build homes, bring up families and contribute to its welfare through their practical labours. And they are to resist the blandishments of those who would call them to resistance and rebellion. God still has Israel's welfare in his own plans. In due time, they will return to the land from which they have so recently been cast out. But for now, their task is not to seek to bring that day forward, but to be good and active citizens where they have found themselves.

The Christian life is always one of exile. Our citizenship is of that kingdom which Jesus proclaimed. Like the Israelites of old, we seek to keep faithful to God in a place that has laws and culture which may pledge allegiance to other powers: money, celebrity or sex. The temptation to opt out, to form and remain within our pure Christian subcultures, is as powerful now as it was in Jeremiah's day. Yet through Jeremiah, God calls us to engagement, to care about the well-being of where we are: to feed the hungry, tend the sick, house the homeless; to speak out against injustice and care for the earth on which we stand. He calls some among us to take up leadership roles in business, charity, church and politics. Such a life brings challenges, requires compromises and necessitates collaboration across boundaries of faith. But through such a life, God will ensure our welfare; and our faith will, at last, be vindicated.

3 Living with the neighbours

Leviticus 19:1–18

The command to 'love your neighbour as yourself' is sometimes assumed to have come from Jesus himself. However, as this passage makes clear, it is taken directly from the Old Testament. The book of Leviticus offers a compendium of practical wisdom about how a society can be constructed and made to work under God. It is couched in terms of the law being given directly by God to Moses, ahead of the Israelites entering the promised land. However, only part of it relates directly to how the people honour and worship God. Much could be applied to any tribe of that era, seeking the necessary order and discipline to manage disputes and to flourish. There are simple suggestions, such as leaving some of the crop in your fields for the poor to find and collect. There is good hygiene advice, such as to not eat food that has been cooked too long ago. All these are mixed in with the big themes of the ten commandments, commands to honour parents and not steal others' property.

In Luke 10, the command to love one's neighbour is quoted by a lawyer in conversation with Jesus. It provokes the story of the good Samaritan, one of the most famous of all the parables that Jesus told. The question put to Jesus by the lawyer picks up the fact that 'neighbour' is not defined in Leviticus. Perhaps the desire to give it a clear specification is driven by a wish to really answer the opposite question: 'Who is NOT my neighbour?' Whom do I have no neighbourly obligations towards? But Leviticus offers no help there. Instead, it offers the image of a highly relational society, where people encounter each other face-to-face. And it uses, in the concept of neighbour, a word that contains an essential parity and impartiality. If I am your neighbour, then you are equally mine. Also in this passage, the neighbour is one over whose behaviour I might be called to exercise judgement. I must do so impartially, unswayed by the wealth or poverty of the person before me, blind to any hierarchy that might place one of us above the other. These are the sorts of behaviours and attitudes towards the neighbour that can be summed up in both Old Testament and New, in that profoundly relational and non-hierarchical word 'love', to which Christians are called.

4 Judgement and justice

One of the strongest and most recurrent themes of scripture is that of justice. The law sets out right and wrong, but justice is the system by which behaviours are rewarded or punished. One is powerless without the other. Either on earth or in heaven, the act of judgement has to be seen to occur and the appropriate consequences to follow. If justice is not seen in this world, then a day of judgement must follow, when God raises the dead to reward or rejection.

In today's passage, Luke sets two stories side by side. The first is a call to perseverance. There would have been little incentive for the judge to spend time on the case of a widow, a person of limited influence and means. And yet her very persistence results in his hearing her complaint and giving her justice. How much more ready is God, the very fount of justice, to hear the cry of his people! In the second story, we read of a person overly quick to come to judgement, and to judge others unfavourably by comparison with himself. Unknowingly, his judgementalism has opened him up to receive condemnation, rather than forgiveness, from God.

Ultimate judgement, the Bible tells us, belongs to God. Yet human beings are called both to execute temporal justice formally, through courts and juries, and to judge situations in everyday life. The key to handling such situations lies in distinguishing between the pursuit of justice and the act of judgement. Justice is something to which we are called; it should be a hallmark of all our engagements with the world around us. For Anglicans, such as myself, the summons to combat injustice through word and deed forms the fourth of our global Five Marks of Mission. But the act of judging others is something we should approach with trepidation, as even Jesus does. We should especially beware of seeking to pass judgement in order to count others as less worthy or valuable than ourselves.

Is it truly healthy that some our most popular TV programmes are ones where the viewers are invited to observe and assess other individuals carrying out some task, be it dancing or singing? My suspicion is that too much of the entertainment value seems to be about finding fault with the performances of the competitors, on whom we then pass judgement by voting them out of the competition.

5 Living as part of creation

Genesis 2:4–23

The second account of creation in the book of Genesis is radically different from the first. It begins not with emptiness but with the earth already fashioned, though as yet without life. God makes a man and sets him on the land. He creates plants and trees for him to till and tend, and the whole range of living creatures to be his companions. Yet the work is only complete with the making of the woman, the one who will be the true mate and partner of Adam. Woman and man form the bookends; between their creation all else is made. Together, they will nurture and maintain the garden on behalf of the God who will walk in it and speak with them, and for the well-being of all of creation.

The notions of humanity being made especially in God's image and having dominion over the earth, while prominent in Genesis 1, are absent from this less dramatic, much more pastoral account. It places us clearly within, not above, creation, to tend the earth as those who live in harmony with our fellow creatures. That there are limits to the extent of humanity's authority is made explicit by God warning the man that he will be punished if he eats any of the fruit of the tree in the garden's centre.

Responsibility for the well-being of creation does not end with the man and woman's expulsion from Eden; it just becomes harder work. It persists to this day, at the very core of our calling, even though many of us live at a much greater physical and emotional distance from our fellow creatures. Where we differ is that we are both far more aware of the physical limits of the earth and more capable of acting in ways that risk permanent damage to it. With that 'knowledge of good and evil' comes greater responsibility.

In the 19th century, as western explorers first reached new territories in Africa and Australasia, some hoped to rediscover the original garden from which Adam and Eve had been expelled, hidden away in some remote corner of the globe, now at last to be opened up again for human habitation. But there is no way back to Eden. Instead, we are challenged to make this whole earth a sustainable habitat for the descendants of all God's creatures, to the end of time.

6 Protection or space to flourish?

The people of Israel come back again and again in the Old Testament to the imagery of shepherds and their flocks. It's a theme picked up by Jesus in parables such as the lost sheep (Matthew 18:12–14), and in his description of himself as the good shepherd (John 10:1–18). The wealth of biblical Israel, much like that of medieval England, owed much to the flourishing of its flocks. Where else to turn for such evocative images? Yet perhaps the sheer power of some of those images has overstressed the role of shepherd as protector against harm and evil, to the neglect of other dimensions.

The biblical shepherd does far more than ward off thieves and predators. He guides and leads the flock to pasture and to water; he provides places to rest and a feast to enjoy; all as the sheep make their way towards a dwelling place he has ready for them. Under his care, the flock grows and flourishes, strong and healthy. The life of the sheep is not primarily focused on the need to ward off constant threat but on abundant food, fresh water and space to dwell in peace. This is the context in which the shepherd can leave ninety-nine sheep to fend on their own while he goes off to search for the one missing.

There are good, evolutionary reasons why we as human beings tend to focus our attention on the most urgent and immediate threat or challenge that faces us. Our distant ancestors, spotting a lion or bear heading towards them, would have needed just such a single-minded approach in order to survive long enough to produce descendants. Yet to cast our lives as a constant series of crises, from which we seek God's power to deliver us, or errors, from which we need him to rescue us, fails to do justice to the biblical imagery of shepherd and flock.

We live in a world that is bewilderingly complex, one where Christians do indeed face constant challenges, in societies where we as subject to anything from persecution to disdain, while temptations multiply. But today's psalm suggests that we should live confidently, defined more by God's promises than by our problems. We are those whom God loves and guides, whom he supplies with their needs and for whom he has a place.

Guidelines

This week's reflections have focused on the challenge of being a Christian, and part of a church, within a secular society. From the moment of creation onwards, our religion is centred not simply on the private realm of our beliefs and prayers, but on the imperative of being a blessing to God's whole creation. We live under secular authority and can also be called to participate in its administration. I am privileged to know a number of men and women who live under the vows of a religious community. From them, I have learned that the monastic cloister is not a place within which to hide from the world, but a viewing point for it. From the convent cell and chapel, God's earth and its people can be viewed from a greater perspective. They, and the matters that concern them, are then held up before their creator in prayer.

The particular challenges that face a society at a given moment in time will vary, and yet they are underpinned by common themes around authority, justice, community, care for creation and support for the needy, which have themselves changed little in thousands of years. In thinking back over these reflections, you might wish to spend some time during your prayers asking God to help you identify two things. First, to guide you to identify a particular issue where you can make a practical difference, either through your own direct efforts or offering moral support and encouragement to someone deeply engaged. And second, to raise your awareness of some concern that you can bring more to the centre of your pattern of intercessory prayer.

1 Living in hope

Romans 5:1–11

The apostle Paul mentions hope 45 times; 15 of these occur in the epistle to the Romans. Along with faith and love, it is one of the three things he tells the church in Corinth will last forever. He has already introduced the concept in Romans 4, referring to the hope that Abraham had in God's promise that he would be father to many nations. But now in Romans 5, having completed his long assertion of justification by faith, he is ready to explore it more fully.

Hope looks forward. It is about our destiny in Christ; we shall enter into the glory of God. In Romans 8, Paul will assert that hope must be in things 'not yet seen'. We have not reached that destiny, as he reminds the church in Thessalonica, for our resurrection is yet to come. Meanwhile, sure grounds for hope lie in what God has already accomplished in Jesus Christ. As Paul sets out here, it is the combination of the crucifixion and resurrection of Jesus that first reconciles us to God, then affirms our eternal promise. That promise, he will say in Romans 8, is offered to the whole of creation.

Between the resurrection of Jesus and the fulfilment of all God's plans, we are invited to live in hope. For me, this is about living with a confidence that God's ultimate purposes will prevail and that we are invited to play a part in that fulfilment of his will. It gives our own lives and work a purposefulness. We may not know exactly how our words and deeds will be knitted into God's greater work, but they will be. And even when we get things wrong, our failings will not be allowed to deny that glorious destiny to any of God's creation. Moreover, hope invites us to look forward more than backward. Christian faith is not nostalgia for better times in the past, when the world was simpler. It's about running the race set before us, as Paul memorably puts it both to the Corinthian church and to Timothy, our eyes set on what lies ahead.

Hope is a light that may burn at its brightest when all around appears dark, even when tempted to despair. We glance briefly back, to the saving deeds of Christ, and then turn forward to face our destiny.

2 Living in one body

1 Corinthians 12:12–31

We should be eternally grateful to the early church in Corinth for getting so many things wrong that the apostle Paul had to write at length and often to them. His words of encouragement and admonition echo down the succeeding 20 centuries. We have as much to learn from them today as did those who read his epistles whilst the ink was barely dry.

The Corinthian church was divided into factions. Some of that was around social status – when they gathered together, the wealthy would eat heartily while the poor watched on. Some of it was around what today we might call churchmanship – those who put great emphasis on the exercise of charismatic gifts being divided from believers whose faith was less effusive and more intellectually rigorous. Both groups looked down on the other as lesser Christians. Paul responds with a series of metaphors, including the body, to call them back to an essential unity. Paradoxically, this requires for their flourishing a high degree of diversity between them. It's a salutary read for any church facing divisive conflicts, as almost all churches always are.

I discovered early on in my Christian discipleship that our hurts and scars, our failures and limitations, are as much the means through which we serve Christ as our gifts and skills. From our weaknesses comes empathy with those who share our failings. Moreover, these should be the factors that draw us to labour alongside others, each filling the gaps in our companions' abilities. I knew God was calling me to ordained ministry both because friends recognised my pastoral skills and because I knew my Christian discipleship needed the extra discipline given by undertaking formal ministry, if I were to flourish as a follower of Christ. Paul's body image serves as a bulwark against the individualism that dominates much present-day western culture, something that would have been unthinkable 2,000 years ago.

The Corinthian church could have easily fragmented along its fracture lines. Paul must have been tempted at times to let them go their separate ways, to form clubs of the like-minded where divisions would be less obvious or painful. But the apostle had something better for them and for us, something he will fully reveal in his next passage to them – the primacy of love.

3 Doers of the word

James 1:19—2:8

The epistle of James is one of my favourite books in the New Testament. I love the way that the author moves backward and forward between the very core of Christian belief and practical human behaviour. To James, proclamations of faith are empty and false if they do not bear fruit in actions. We are to be not merely hearers but 'doers of the word' (v. 22). We may enjoy rousing sermons, be lifted to ecstasy by worship songs or be caught up in heaven when receiving the sacrament. Yet if none of these impact on what we do after our act of worship is over, we are like someone who has had a mirror held up so they can see their true features but then immediately forgets what they look like. It's a huge theological point, and followed immediately by a reminder to curb the excesses of our tongues and exercise care towards orphans and widows. James takes his own medicine: he doesn't leave us just with big, theoretical concepts; they must be harnessed by practice straight away.

The first part of James 2 takes us on the return journey. We begin with a practical issue of human behaviour, the tendency to favour the rich at the expense of the poor. James' simple example is all too recognisable, even 2,000 years on from when he wrote it. And yet to behave in the natural human way is to refute the very things we believe. It is the poor whom God is making rich in faith; they will be the true inheritors of God's kingdom. By contrast, the rich are most commonly our abusers and oppressors, the ones most likely to despise and revile the name of Jesus. Our deeds should not be grounded in standard human behaviour, but in the central command of God to love our neighbour as we love our own selves. The journey back from the particular to the very essence of the faith is complete.

This movement between the particular and the deepest truths lies at the core of what is often called 'reflective practice'. We hold up the mirror of our faith to ourselves, examine what we see in its reflection and then remember and apply the insights we have gleaned. That way, our future actions and our faith become ever more closely aligned. It should lie at the heart of all of our lives.

4 A new thing

Isaiah 42:1–13

The second part of the book of Isaiah is one of the most consistently forward-looking sections of the Bible. The author's focus is not on what God has done for his people in the past, nor on what he is accomplishing in the present; it's on what new and surprising things God will do in the future. From the earliest days, Christians have seen these chapters as pointing towards the coming of Christ; they have been much mined for church readings in Advent and at Christmas. That God should send his own Son, to take the form of a servant and enter his creation, is not the only way of reading these passages. But for those who catch such a glimpse in Isaiah's words, this is foretelling something entirely new and unprecedented: something far better than all that has come before.

One of the consistent ideological norms of ancient society, whether Jewish, Greek or Roman, was that the general trajectory of the world was downhill. It's played out in the steadily decreasing lifespans recorded in the books of Genesis and Exodus, from almost a thousand years to our present mortal limits. Philosophical ideas and systems would be compared and judged less on their intrinsic merit than on the length of their ancestry. I suspect it's a way of thinking that owes much to the fact that prominent teachers are often older people, who project their own personal physical decline on to the world around them and its history: 'Things were better when I was young!'

Caught up in such views, Christians have often seen Isaiah's words as prophesying only a temporary reversal of this downward trend. After Easter and Pentecost, things can return to the norm of decay. But Isaiah's vision takes us beyond the coming of the Christ, to a God who will continue to break anew into our world until the end of time itself. If we fail to see and embrace the new things God is doing in our own place and time, we are little better than those who failed to recognise the promised Messiah even as he walked among them. However old we are, we need to reject the notion that change is something to view with suspicion. Instead, let us welcome the new opportunities and challenges God places before us, both in the church and in the world.

5 Weak and strong

Romans 14:13–23

In today's passage, the apostle Paul takes the example of food sacrificed to idols to show how something entirely innocuous to one Christian may be damaging to another. The strong believer knows that idols are nothing, and hence no harm can come to them from partaking in the meal. However, for the weaker believer, even observing another Christian act in such a way could damage their faith. Paul's solution is for the strong to refrain from behaviour that might cause another to sin.

Coming from Paul, who is such a strong advocate of the freedom we have in Christ, these are words that merit careful consideration. There are two aspects that I find especially challenging.

First, is what Paul says purely valid at the level of individual behaviour, or should his words guide us in framing the way we structure our church and our society? Alcohol and gambling provide topical examples. The majority of us in society are able to drink socially and to place the occasional bet in ways that provide harmless enjoyment. However, a small minority of those who indulge become addicted, often ruining both their own lives and the lives of those dear to them. How far, then, should these activities be regulated or banned? How do we balance small benefits to the many against severe harm to the few? How do we tread the tightrope between the Wild West and the nanny state?

Equally tricky, though, is how we avoid falling foul of what might be called the tyranny of victimhood. There are many examples where those who self-define as the weaker argue that, because of what they have suffered, others must now accede to their demands. In reality, they are claiming a position of strength. Often observed in political conflicts, it is not unknown in religious disputes, too. Christians and their churches can be pressured to forgo their freedom in Christ in order to conform to the sensitivities of powerful lobbies that clothe themselves in a pretended weakness or victimhood. Where such efforts succeed, the result is often a deeper mistreatment of the truly weak. Yet, crucially, this is the antithesis of what Paul advocates. The restraint he commends is one entered into voluntarily, never the result of manipulation or coercion.

6 Dying well

Luke 2:22–40

The older I get, the more I am drawn to the story of Simeon and Anna greeting the infant Jesus and his parents in the Jerusalem temple. It's a story of long lives, lived in godly fashion, as they come towards the end of their span. Out of that depth of experience and devotion, they recognise that Israel's Messiah is here, in the very temple dedicated to the God who has promised them a Saviour. They respond by praising God for something they will not live to see come to fruition. It will be another 30 years before Jesus begins to proclaim the gospel. Meanwhile, Simeon and Anna can die content, a good death.

At the heart of the story, both Anna and Simeon speak. Crucially, their subject is not the past deeds of Israel or even their own history. Their words are about the new work that God will accomplish through Jesus. It will carry a cost – a sword will pierce Mary's soul – but that work will be both a light to the Gentiles and the glory of Israel. The future which Simeon and Anna have glimpsed will not be a return to the past. It will be new and radically different. Even the temple itself has only a few more decades, less than the span of their lifetimes, before it will be destroyed. They offer no sadness at this passing, merely a delight that God is at work among them. May we all attain such a good death as theirs!

Reaching a good death is, however, not just a matter for individuals; it is equally important for groups and institutions. But, if anything, this seems even harder. Many years ago, I was involved with a church that had had to take the painful decision to close the Sunday school. I remember someone asking what the woman who had begun that work, decades ago, would think if she were still alive to see us ending it. My response was that she would be grateful for all it had achieved and would wonder what new possibilities for working with children would come in its place, now we had freed up space and energy. The parish gave thanks for what had been and allowed it to end gracefully. It wasn't long before a new and very different group started.

Guidelines

Over these last few days, we have explored some of the challenges that face us as Christians seeking to live lives faithful to God, in fellowship with the wider church. We have seen how the church, no less than the society around it, can be a place where tensions exist, as different groups and individuals press their opinions and agendas. I hope that we can be encouraged by the fact that this is in itself nothing new. Those first churches we read about in the New Testament are beset by similar issues. Yet the writers of the various epistles that have come down to us urge their readers to understand each other better, to serve each other generously and to show all this in deed as much as in word.

We have seen, too, how those first churches grapple with the newness of their faith: a faith not simply new to them as individuals, but new because God himself is doing things he has never done before. They have been freed from the bonds of former rules and past practices, whether they are from Jewish or pagan stock. Like a prisoner released from jail after a sentence of many years, or indeed anyone newly set free, they struggle to identify where the new boundaries are. How are they to live outside their old walls? Some will always seek to return to their former regime, like the cobbler released from the Bastille in Dickens' *A Tale of Two Cities*. Others will throw off all constraints and descend to licentiousness.

Whether we have been believers as long as Simeon and Anna, or are new converts greedily devouring every new thing we can find, may we pray over these next few days for God to help us find that path between the old and the new, between freedom and good order. And, if you have the opportunity to help others in their journey of faith, pray for the wisdom to guide them gently along that same way too.

FURTHER READING

David F. Ford, *The Shape of Living: Spiritual directions for everyday life* (Fount, 1997).

Kenneth Leech, *The Social God* (Sheldon Press, 1981).

John Sentamu (ed.), *On Rock or Sand? Firm foundations for Britain's future* (SPCK, 2015).

David Walker, *God's Belongers: How people engage with God today and how the church can help* (BRF, 2017).

Justin Welby, *Reimagining Britain: Foundations for hope* (Bloomsbury, 2018).

Ecclesiastes: a book of inconvenient truths

Peter Hatton

It's a privilege to be able to share this wonderful book with you. I've been exploring the riches of Israel's wisdom literature in academic contexts for 20 years. But I am also a pastor (25 years as a Methodist circuit minister), so I know the value of this literature outside the academy to instruct us, provoke us and point us to Christ.

Some three millennia ago, a tale was told in the ancient Near East about a king who, it seemed, had everything anyone could wish for. Rich and wise, he had tasted all the world's pleasures. Yet they counted for nothing because he knew that, one day, he would die and lose them all. So he embarked on a quest to see if life had any meaning in the face of death.

Sound familiar? If we know the biblical book of Ecclesiastes, we might be forgiven for thinking that it's described above! It may then come as a surprise to learn that it also fits another classic of ancient literature, the epic of Gilgamesh. Whether the author(s) of Ecclesiastes knew the (almost certainly older) Gilgamesh is uncertain. Intriguingly, the unusual metaphor of 'a threefold cord is not quickly broken' of Ecclesiastes 4:12 is also found in Gilgamesh. Be that as it may, the similarities are significant.

Both Ecclesiastes and Gilgamesh ask questions that have been posed down the ages and remain relevant today. Our lives are short and, even if we prosper, they are often filled with toil and trouble; and then we die! Does any of it make sense? Is it not just absurd? Even those who – like the author(s) of Ecclesiastes – believe in God, ask such questions and find that there are no easy answers.

For those who think the scriptures offer facile comfort to gullible people ('pie in the sky when you die'), Ecclesiastes comes as a bracing shock. This disconcerting book testifies that faith in God doesn't tell us to shut our eyes to reality, but rather encourages us to probe its deepest mysteries with a bold, determined persistence.

Unless otherwise stated, Bible quotations are taken from the ESV.

1 Gathering wisdom

Ecclesiastes 1

Whose words are these (v. 1)? 'They are Solomon's', is the traditional answer. That, however, is difficult to square with Ecclesiastes 2:7, which implies that there have been many (Israelite) kings in Jerusalem before the writer. Moreover, does the title 'teacher' or 'preacher' (v. 2) really fit Solomon? In fact, both these attempts to render the underlying Hebrew word, *Qohelet*, don't do it justice. It is from the root *qahal*, 'to gather', and so it might be translated 'one who gathers' (or 'collects'). Accordingly, Solomon, who 'spoke' a collection of proverbs (1 Kings 4:32), and to whom the authorship of the book of Proverbs is ascribed, might be back in the frame; but the word is in a feminine form. So a very literal rendering is 'she who gathers'.

This makes little sense until we remember that, in Proverbs, Wisdom is personified as a woman. Accordingly, the opening words of Ecclesiastes contain a daring claim; that in the words of this 'son of David', we hear Wisdom herself speaking. If so, this is puzzling, for the final words of this chapter (vv. 16–18) seem to state that there is little point in being wise. Why would the confident Wisdom of, for instance, Proverbs 3:13–18 say this? Well, perhaps because of the shallow belief – as current in modern times as it was in ancient Jerusalem – that our cleverness and ingenuity will enable us to overcome every problem we meet.

Against such arrogant nonsense, Wisdom asserts the great truth that 'all is vanity' (v. 2). Here again, an enquiry into the original Hebrew will help us. The word is *hebel*, which means literally something like 'a breath' or 'a vapour', something that lasts only for a few seconds before it gets blown away. So Qohelet proclaims that any human belief in the ultimate importance of our toil and our strivings is 'madness and folly' (v. 17), mocked by the vast eons of time (vv. 4–11) in which our little lives are lost.

Moreover, *hebel* is the name rendered into English as 'Abel', who was the first person to die in the Bible, murdered in a senseless, absurd quarrel (Genesis 4:8–16). Our lives are, all too often, 'nasty, brutish and short'. We may not like this, but, says Qohelet, it is true and we must not forget it.

2 Toil and trouble

In the last chapter, we saw that Qohelet puts his (or her) words in the mouth of a powerful, wise king. It is this persona that allows her to run what we might call a thought experiment.

What if we had everything anyone could possibly want? We might day-dream about what we would do, were we rich and clever, but what if we actually thought through carefully what might happen? Qohelet does just that: no human joy is denied to the king (vv. 1–10), yet his heart is not dulled and corrupted by these pleasures (v. 9) and he is able to reflect upon their ultimate worth (vv. 11, 17).

In so doing, he comes to some stark conclusions about how truly happy such pleasures might make him. They are 'vanity' (v. 1 – that word *hebel* again); a 'striving after wind' (v. 17) – a strenuous pursuit of what cannot be caught. Yes, being clever can lead to worldly success and is valuable in its own right (v. 14); but, so what? In the end, anything that we have gained, experienced and learned is meaningless in the face of death (vv. 14–15). As the saying goes, 'You can't take it with you.'

The life of the workaholic is particularly absurd. Those who toil cease-lessly, denying themselves (and their loved ones) the simple joys of human existence, even depriving themselves of sleep, are making themselves mis-erable (vv. 18–23). Ironically, when they drop dead of a stress-induced heart attack, their hard-gotten wealth will pass to someone who never lifted a finger to earn it (v. 21).

Interestingly, it is at this point that Qohelet brings in God (vv. 24–26). From what we have seen so far, in spite of the fleeting reference to the deity in 1:13, we might be tempted to think the book offers us a stern morality but has little to do with religion. We shall see that, as we go on, this is not the case. God is linked here (v. 24) with a glimmer of hope that human existence might not be completely bleak, but he is also ultimately responsible for the futility which mocks even those who have wisdom and manage to avoid the folly of sin (v. 26).

3 'When true simplicity is gain'd'

Ecclesiastes 3:1–8 is, perhaps, the most well-known passage in the whole book, sometimes read at funerals, where, perhaps, people want to affirm that the life of the deceased (and indeed all human life) had some sort of shape and purpose. Of course, we know of exceptions; we might say, for instance, that 'X died before their time', but even this implies that what was ordained for them, somehow, didn't come about. If this is the case, the passage, although it does not explicitly mention God, somehow brings him in (as the one who ordains everything).

Certainly, Qohelet wants to link the notion of a life in which there is a time for everything with the God who affirms the beauty of creation (compare v. 11a and Genesis 1:10, 12, 18, etc.). However, as he does so, Qohelet knows that there are profound mysteries about God's purposes that we will never understand (v. 11b). He may have ordered the creation wisely and well, but it now contains puzzling disorder – for instance, wickedness and corruption instead of righteousness and justice (v. 16).

Why does God allow this? Well, perhaps so that we don't take ourselves too seriously; so that we don't protest too quickly when matters are not as we think they should be, lest we arrogantly assume that 'it's all about us' (or even worse 'all about me'). We need to remember that we die, as animals do (vv. 18–20), and that any belief in a life after death for humans is a matter of faith, not of certain knowledge (v. 21).

If there is a time for everything but we can't find out when that is, what's the point? Should we not just despair and die? Not so; if we are humble enough to accept our limitations, life offers us daily many opportunities for simple joys and fulfilment. Meals with friends and family, a job well done (vv. 12–13, 22) – these are the pleasures, indeed the delights, open to those who see through the folly of self-importance and overweening ambition. Those mindful of the simple things will value them above the bubbles of wealth and reputation.

4 Discords

Ecclesiastes never lets us rest in easy certainties. The book has sought repeatedly to break down our satisfied complacency. But if we think we've got our heads round its teaching by this point, we need to think again.

Having just said that there are some simple pleasures that offer real consolation (3:12–13), we now hear that, given the injustice in the world, it's better not to have been born (vv. 1–3; compare Job 3:16–19). And, if we thought on the basis of 3:22 that a job well done might offer us some consolation, now we are told 'all toil and all skill in work come from a man's envy of his neighbour' (v. 4).

This is, perhaps, the manner of the book. Sometimes, it seems, Qohelet believes he can only get his point across by exaggerating.

Yet immediately after he has gone so over the top, he seems anxious to nuance and pull back. He is not urging us to be so idle that we destroy ourselves (v. 5). No, once again, he seems to have in mind the workaholism that cuts us off from real relationship. Life isolated from other people cannot flourish; friendship, collaboration and even co-belligerence are essential things (vv. 8–11).

Once again, we are dealing with the manner of the book. Qohelet seemingly cannot assert something without immediately thinking of its opposite and, as passionately as before, advancing that contrary opinion.

If we are seeking precise logic, we will find this highly frustrating. However, we may read Ecclesiastes more intelligently if we respond to it imaginatively, perhaps in the way we might respond to a complex piece of music where strong themes are sounded that then generate other, discordant elements. We are not offered easy resolutions and simple conclusions, but does this not resemble the way life often comes to us, full of complexities, even contradictions?

In any event, this chapter closes with an example of how even the most amazing achievement – the scaling of the heights of power by one who started at the bottom – leaves no long-lasting legacy (vv. 14–16). This is a theme we have already touched on; it will sound again.

5 Restraint

If Qohelet's sombre view on life strikes a discordant note in a modern world accustomed to whistling happy tunes in the face of its fears, then his religious insights may sound harsh to a contemporary church that often loves to accentuate the positive. God, for Qohelet, is not a cuddly teddy bear whose main task is to comfort us; nor, he thinks (vv. 2–3) does God wish to be worshipped with many words, repetitive singing or wordy liturgies. If we promise him much – that we will, for instance, give him everything we have and are – beware! He may hold us to our word (vv. 4–6).

For those who cringe when worship fails to point to God's awesome mystery and sheer otherness, this stress on the need for moderation, respect, even caution, when approaching him (v. 1) may be refreshing. Qohelet warns against a flawed religiosity that confuses spirituality with superstition and verbosity with true worship (vv. 2–3, 7). His judgement on such fantasies (v. 7) is crushing: it is 'vanity' – *hebel* again – and here 'ludicrous self-importance' might be a good translation. The true worshipper will choose silence over loud expressions of the outward shows of religion and will prefer deep reverence to bouncy displays of emotion.

As in the temple, so in the palace and in the marketplace; caution and restraint are Qohelet's watchwords. His apparent lack of passion for social justice (vv. 8–9) will be found deeply disturbing by sections of today's church; his scathing observations on anything approaching the 'prosperity gospel' (vv. 10–17) will offend yet others.

'Count your blessings; be content with your lot' summarises his advice in verses 18–20. This counsel might be seen as oppressive. Has Qohelet no concern for the sorrows of the world? Should we simply resign ourselves to injustice? We might respond by noting the deep feeling of compassion implicit in, for instance, verse 17 and, more generally, by reflecting that a culture of dissatisfaction and complaint may sometimes cause more problems than it solves. Patient acceptance can be as much an expression of true faith as passionate protest against the infringement of our (or even others') rights.

6 Enjoy it, if you can

Qohelet may advocate acceptance of our lot, but he is well aware that few can follow his advice. Indeed, contentment is a grace, a gift of God (v. 2), and many people are not able to receive it. Accordingly, a state of restless dissatisfaction is normal even for those who seem to have everything (vv. 2–3; we are reminded of the king in Ecclesiastes 1—2). This is, once again, *hebel* (v. 23). Here, the word points to an absurdity in human life, to our restless search for satisfaction, which we will never find, because we always want more, no matter how much we already have (v. 7). Trapped by our desires into lives that offer us no lasting gain, it would be better for us had we never been born (vv. 3–5). What's more, even if we were able, somehow, to prolong our lifespans beyond Methuselah's (Genesis 5:25–27), all of us still have to 'go to the one place' (v. 6); that is, we must all die.

In verse 9, we find an enigmatic phrase usually rendered as 'the wandering of the appetite [or desire]', and this is stated to be inferior to the 'sight of the eyes'. This doesn't make much sense. However, an alternative translation would be 'the going of the soul' (the word *nephesh* can mean both 'desire' and 'that in us which desires', i.e. our 'life force' or 'soul'). In that case, the phrase is another euphemism for death and is contrasted with life, where we see the light.

So, once again, we are confronted with a harsh paradox. On the one hand, we are all – rich and poor, wise and foolish – plagued by appetites we cannot satisfy; yet, for all that, to be alive and see the light of day is better than 'to die, and go we know not where' (*Measure for Measure*, Act III, Scene 1). Tired of living and scared of dying, our situation is *hebel*, absurd (v. 9).

A final twist is that there is only one whom we can blame for this state of affairs: God. In a phrase that reminds us of Job, humanity 'is not able to dispute with one stronger than he' (v. 10; compare Job 9:3, 19). If there's a plan, we are not privy to it . We can rage against the 'vanity' of our existence, but it will do us no good (vv. 11–12).

Guidelines

If you have access to the internet, you should be able to track down a clip of Paul Robeson, the great African American actor, scholar and singer, singing 'Ol' Man River' from the film *Showboat* (1936). The song could be a musical summary of Ecclesiastes. Robeson's sensitive interpretation of its lyrics brings out the pain-filled paradox of his people's experience of life, in which there is so much oppression and from which not even death can offer release.

'I'm tired of living and scared of dying,' Robeson sings, but in such a way that he makes us aware of a compassion and humanity behind the pessimism; it is deeply moving and, in a curious way, uplifting. My intuition as a pastor, and a teacher of those called to be pastors, is that if we always seek 'to accentuate the positive and eliminate the negative' (Jonny Mercer, 1994) in our presentation of the gospel, we do it a grave disservice. I was astonished to learn that, in a massive online catalogue of some 80,000 Christian songs, arranged by genre, no category exists for laments! Indeed, as one who worships in a variety of churches, I note that we rarely sing with the psalmist, 'How long, O Lord? Will you forget me forever?' (Psalm 13:1), or admit with Qohelet, 'It is an unhappy business that God has given the children of men to be busy with' (Ecclesiastes 1:13).

Of course, our worship should be filled with the praises of the extraordinary God who sent his only Son to die for us and whose Spirit fills us in life's trials; but within that praise, should we not also sound the note to whose truth Qohelet testifies: the note of bewilderment, of loss, of what we might call 'sanctified pessimism'? If we seek to listen to 'the whole counsel of God', then we will not edit out that note.

Our own devotions will be more authentic if, in them, we face and pray through those situations that do not easily fit into a glib, Panglossian account of the world. What's more, we may find that such a robust, unblinkered faith is surprisingly attractive to those who dismiss Christianity as unreal and trivial.

Listen to Robeson sing and pray for the people who, today, lift heavy loads and are 'soon forgotten'. If you count yourself one of them, tell God your complaints. Psalm 88, or one of the older hymns that allow us to express grief and sorrow, may help you express your feelings.

1 Memento mori

Ecclesiastes 7

Ecclesiastes, Proverbs and Job form the wisdom books of the Old Testament, books that share some common concerns and much in the way of vocabulary and forms of expression. Ecclesiastes 7:1–13 is a point at which Ecclesiastes seems close in terms of form to parts of Proverbs, particularly the collection of pithy, one-line sayings in Proverbs 10:1—22:16.

There are similarities in content, too. Verses 5–6 and 8–13 advocate the sort of teachable, patient conduct enjoined upon us throughout Proverbs. However, Qohelet's distinctive emphasis sounds in some of the other verses here. Surprise, surprise – these are paradoxical, provocative statements. It is, it seems, better to go to a wake than a birthday party (vv. 1–2).

I have had the privilege of walking with many people through terminal illness. One cannot generalise, but I have often been humbled by the way the dying can delight in life – in small pleasures, in pictures that evoke memories of good times in the past, in the company of loved ones – even as life ebbs away. Sometimes, only as we face the fact that we must lose life do we see it as the precious gift it is. Qohelet suggests that we should embrace our own mortality daily, value the life we have now and live it to the full. And this we should do even though, as the rest of the chapter proclaims (vv. 15–18, 25), so much in life still puzzles us. We may also be puzzled by the rampant misogyny of verses 26–28. Perhaps some of any offence may be mitigated by Qohelet's own feminine aspects.

Martin Luther loved Ecclesiastes. His doctrine of salvation by grace alone inclined him to read verse 20 as a proof text for total depravity. However, what really drew Luther to the book was what he saw as its life-affirming message. Once we deconstruct the myth of our own wisdom and goodness, we are freed to live the life of faith, totally reliant on God's grace, delighting in his gifts to us and not in our own self-important 'righteousness' (v. 16).

2 Think it through

We will have gathered by now that Ecclesiastes is not afraid of repeating itself. Here, we meet again several familiar themes: the caution with which we are to handle the powerful (vv. 2–5, 9); our inability to foresee events or fully understand God's ways (vv. 7, 16–17); the inevitability and unpredictability of death (v. 8); life's unfairness – that bad things happen to good people and vice versa (v. 14); the wisdom of enjoying the good life when we can (v. 15).

However, other statements in the chapter seem to take issue with these teachings. Thus the explicit statement in verses 10–13 – that, in the end, the wicked will get their comeuppance – does not sit well with verse 14's claim that the righteous can suffer pain, or even be punished, while the wicked may flourish. Is Wisdom something that glorifies us and raises us up (v. 1)? Or is it a humble tool whose usefulness is limited by our lack of foreknowledge (v. 17)? These contradictions are not the first in the book, nor the last.

Could it be that Qohelet is prompting us to examine the popular folk wisdom that we can default to thoughtlessly? So, for instance, hearing of the misfortune of someone we think is selfish and hard-hearted, we might say, 'What goes around, comes around!' – the essence of verses 10–13, more or less. However, verse 14 reminds us of the inconvenient truth that some hard-hearted selfish people thrive and go with years and honour to the grave, while some compassionate, just people die lonely and impoverished. Once again, we may know sayings a bit like that – for example, 'It's the rich what gets the pleasure; it's the poor what gets the blame.'

Indeed, proverbial folk wisdom often contradicts itself (as the biblical book of Proverbs knows very well, Proverbs 26:4–5). Qohelet seeks to make contradictory elements of this wisdom confront each other and so to challenge us to work things out for ourselves. Yet it may be, as verses 16–17 state, that final answers to life's contradictions are not available; it is better to remain uncertain than cling to false certainties.

3 'And yet to times in hope my verse shall stand'

Ecclesiastes 9

Reading this chapter, it's tempting to say, 'Same!' Qohelet returns again to what we might be quick to dismiss as, by now, his all-too-familiar tropes: the inevitability of death for both sage and simpleton, sinner and saint (vv. 1–6); the paradoxical imperative to make the most of the pleasures we can enjoy and to affirm and celebrate life in the face of death (vv. 7–10); that strength and intelligence may avail us little in the face of chance and fate (vv. 11–12); that even exceptional achievements and public service are forgotten in time's onward rush (vv. 13–16); finally, a panegyric of wisdom with a characteristically laconic observation that throws some doubt on what has just been said (vv. 17–18).

So nothing we have not heard before. Why bother with it?

Well, as Dr Samuel Johnson remarked, 'Men more frequently require to be reminded than informed.' (This may also be true of women.) Given that we tend to default repeatedly to naively positive understandings of scripture and Christian faith, Qohelet repeatedly points us to inconvenient truths we would rather ignore.

Moreover, we should note how these negative, unattractive propositions are, paradoxically, often expressed in memorable, striking, indeed even beautiful ways. There are examples in this chapter of sayings that retain the power to move today:

- 'A living dog is better than a dead lion' (v. 4)

- 'Whatever your hand finds to do, do it with your might' (v. 10)

- 'The race is not to the swift, nor the battle to the strong' (v. 11)

To my mind, these aesthetic qualities of Ecclesiastes are deeply significant. It is ironic that a book whose doctrines may come across as harsh and forbidding can be read with such pleasure for its artistry and poetic power. But then, many of us like to hear the blues sung, or even, perhaps, to sing the blues ourselves. Indeed, there is a deep irony here. True, our author (or perhaps authors) is anonymous, but even as Qohelet proclaims that 'all is vanity' and nothing we do lives after us, his words are still being read and pondered thousands of years after his death. It seems, even by his agnostic standards, there is a sort of immortality after all.

4 Folly ruins everything

Ecclesiastes 10

In our study of Ecclesiastes, we have been following the conventional chapter divisions. These ancient divisions (devised by Archbishop Langton, d. 1228) do not always correspond to units of sense. However, practically any division of the book is going to be somewhat arbitrary and Langton did well in Ecclesiastes, all things considered.

Moreover, this chapter's sayings, many somewhat enigmatic, reveal again that expectations of neat, orderly development are not going to be met by Ecclesiastes (and, indeed, by other books of the Bible). So we are offered observations about folly in verses 1–3, but the next verse seems to be almost entirely unrelated, for it deals with what we should do in the face of the anger of the powerful; then (vv. 5–7), we get a short section on a social world where everything is upside down. There follow verses 8–11, most of which assert the doctrine, found also in Proverbs and the Psalms, that evil brings its own punishment with it – but what do we make of the puzzling verse 11? A further four verses (vv. 12–15) reinforce a by-now-familiar message about the dangers of folly. The chapter concludes with consideration of how rulers should conduct themselves and a warning against speaking in ways that might seem subversive.

Both in form and content, there are further similarities here with the book of Proverbs, which also often seems to flit from topic to topic. However, it is perhaps possible to discern some central concerns raised in the chapter. It can be understood as a meditation in the form of a dialogue about folly and its effects, a theme announced in the first verses, and thereafter we see the effect of folly in many different settings, including the worlds of politics and statecraft. What is true in the home is true in the palace; laziness and corruption lead to misery on both the small and the large scale.

A particularly disturbing message is given in verse 20. It seems that, whatever the political situation that lay behind the writing of Ecclesiastes, there were enough informers around to make free speech dangerous. So prudence is the watchword, but Qohelet hints that such repression is itself a sign of state-sponsored foolishness.

5 Go on, have a flutter!

Ecclesiastes 11

More enigmatic sayings dominate the first half of this chapter (vv. 1–6). Some translators, keen to explain things, interpret verses 1–2 as an encouragement to foreign trade ('send your grain overseas', NET) and risk management ('Divide your merchandise among seven or even eight investments', NET again). These may be plausible applications for readers engaged in commerce, but the more literal renderings – 'cast your bread upon the waters' and 'give a portion to seven, or even to eight' (ESV, following the KJV) – are surely preferable because of their much wider reference and poetic power.

Indeed, Qohelet, in these verses, returns to one of his major themes – that the future is unknown to us and beyond our control – but draws from it an unexpected conclusion. He insists that this cosmic uncertainty must be met with a readiness to take risks, to invest time and energy and resources in things that might fail. Yes, there is no real security in this life and we neither control nor understand some of the most important things in it (v. 5). However, our response should not be passive fatalism but bold activism. Given that he has often recommended caution and prudence (3:22; 4:8; 5:1–2, 10–11; 6:9), this encouragement to live dangerously is, perhaps, surprising. However, from Abram on, those who have responded to God's call have not seen faith as a 'safety-first' policy, but rather have ventured out boldly, trusting that, although not all we undertake will prosper, in the end the harvest will be great.

Characteristically, Qohelet balances this exhortation to boldness with sayings that cool our ardour. Verses 7–10 remind us how brief are the best times in life; that even youth, the time when we are, perhaps, most ready to take risks and to enjoy life to the full, is *hebel*. Old age is coming and, after that, death (v. 8). Moreover, lest we abandon all restraint, we must remember that we will be held to account by God for what we did in the days of our careless youth. Sombre stuff! But then what else did we expect from Qohelet?

6 'It ends with words of Torah'

The chapter division here interrupts the flow of thought, for verses 1–7 contain a sustained meditation on what comes after youth, that is, decline, old age and death. The images here are allusive. Do they refer to the processes of ageing in an individual life (so 'the grinders' in verse 3 could be the teeth), or do they depict, as some commentators think, an apocalyptic end to humanity itself? Perhaps both are simultaneously suggested. Be that as it may, once again, the beauty of the language, its sheer poetic power, brilliantly offsets what is otherwise deeply sombre and pessimistic.

Verse 8 brings us back to the thematic statement which began the book and resounds through it: 'All is *hebel*.'

The conventional scholarly explanation of the last verses in the book (vv. 9–14) is that they are an epilogue offered by an editor (sometimes called the 'frame narrator', as he is held also to have contributed the prologue, 1:1–11). This, supposedly, explains the shift in perspective from the first person to the third, and the evaluative tone of these final words. Personally, I am unconvinced; we are, after all, dealing with an author who is given to self-examination and who often speaks elsewhere in the third person.

That there is, however, a profound shift in perspective in this final section, I don't doubt. Yes, the truth of all that we have just read and its capacity to prod us into different ways of being and thinking are affirmed (vv. 9–12). But no matter how clever we think we have become by reading his words, please let's not add our own twopenny-worth of written wisdom to the material destined for the recycling bin (v. 13; I comfort myself that these are notes, not a book).

However, Qohelet's wisdom is to be set in a wider perspective. The truths to which he has borne witness must be heard, but they must sound within the fear of God and the commandments. This is the 'whole' (in spite of most English versions, the word 'duty' is not found in the Hebrew of verse 13) for humanity. Within this all-encompassing understanding of God's purposes, Qohelet's pessimism can be both included and sanctified, but it must neither dominate nor limit the wider picture.

The final word is with God, judge of all, who, in the end, will bring all that is now hidden to light.

Guidelines

If you went to a cemetery near you, you might notice that some graves bear epitaphs assuring us of the continuing presence of the deceased in memories (e.g. 'never forgotten', 'always in our thoughts'). As belief in 'the life of the world to come' declines, so the consolation of such a tenuous immortality has been grasped at. 'Really?' we might ask, with Qohelet.

But even the most dearly missed are not a constant presence in the minds of the living. Indeed, if someone is unable to stop thinking about a dead loved one, might this not be a sign that the grieving process has some-how been derailed? Is it not more normal and healthy to let go and move on with life? Not, of course, that we forget completely but, as the pain of grief dulls, might not other joys, even other loves, rightly become our focus? Moreover, those who remember us when we are gone will themselves die and, with their deaths, we become even more of a shadowy presence among the living.

A depressing reflection? In God's mercy, it can become a liberating truth, freeing us from pompous ideas about our own importance and indispens-ability, prompting us to live life to the full as it is offered to us every day by a good God. The false gods – career, reputation, number of Twitter followers, prestige, possessions, a concern for 'legacy' – have claimed our devotion and time long enough. If they fall, we can offer our friends and loved ones, as well as those in need and pain, real attention and companionship; we can take pleasure in life's simple joys: a meal, a walk, a job well done.

Qohelet does not speak the whole story of the God who is renewing all things in Christ, but he does speak a word that needs to be heard about the times when God's plan is obscured, hidden. It is a word that needs to be heard.

FURTHER READING

Peter Enns, *Ecclesiastes (The Two Horizons Old Testament Commentary)* (Eerdmans, 2011).

Michael Fox, *A Time to Tear Down and a Time to Build Up: A rereading of Ecclesiastes* (Eerdmans, 1999).

Samuel Johnson, *The Vanity of Human Wishes* (1748 – in his collected works or online).

James Limburg, *Encountering Ecclesiastes: A book for our time* (Eerdmans, 2006).

Cultivating contemplation

Paul Bradbury

Many people, including myself and many of those I know and work alongside, are finding the ancient practices of the contemplative tradition a huge source of sustenance and life in the midst of the pressured, busy and noisy world we live in. The church environment is sadly no exception to the increased pace, volume and anxiety of the modern world. Yet the church has treasures to offer from the testimony of the Bible and the wisdom and experience of the saints. These are treasures which offer a realistic way of embodying a non-anxious and attentive presence in the context of our frenetic world.

This week of notes attempts to offer some biblical foundation and practical wisdom to the task of cultivating an attitude of contemplation within the reality of our life and ministry. Thomas Merton described contemplation as 'the awareness and realisation, even in some sense experience, of what each Christian obscurely believes: "It is no longer I who lives but Christ who lives in me"' (Merton, p. 15). This week, we take a journey to the foundations and practices of contemplation, which is really a life lived in the practice of that truth that the presence of God dwells in us and informs our actions and attitude in all of life.

We begin in the Old Testament, where texts from Proverbs and the Psalms ground contemplation in an honest understanding of our humanity (Proverbs 4:20–27) and in a right view of the sovereignty of God (Psalm 46). Ezekiel (Ezekiel 37:1–6) and then Jesus (Matthew 15:21–28) provide examples of how contemplation is embodied through relinquishment and the acknowledgement of our own limitations as human beings. Finally, we explore how the contemplative life can grow in us through discipline and practice (Philippians 3:12–21), and inform our posture towards our engagement with the world (Acts 17:16–34).

Unless otherwise stated, Bible quotations are taken from the NIV.

1 Guard your heart

Proverbs 4:20–27

The opening chapters of Proverbs lay out the value and importance of wisdom, as a set of characteristics and a lifelong pursuit. They may well have started life as the teaching given to students in a wisdom school. This particular passage may form part of a series of teaching preparing the young students to leave the school and continue to pursue wisdom in daily life.

These are concluding teachings, valedictory words that encapsulate the key elements of the longer discourse that has gone before. The teacher urges his students to continue to hold these teachings closely (vv. 20–21), because they are the source and generator of life (v. 22). The teacher goes on to emphasise the holistic importance of wisdom by employing a list of the parts of the body – our entire being is to be engaged in the pursuit of wisdom (vv. 23–27).

Foremost in this list is the heart. 'Above all else, guard your heart' (v. 23). The heart in Hebrew thought was not just a synonym for love or passion, as it is sometimes reduced to in our culture. It was the centre of physical and spiritual life. It could refer to physical strength and thought, as well as emotions. It was the place where these elements of our humanity integrated. It was the word that located this mysterious complexity of our being, which connects with our will to form our behaviour.

In a world that is accelerated, anxious and acquisitive, when the pressure to act, to achieve and to acquire makes us frenetic and reactionary, these are powerful words. 'Guard your heart' – protect this precious mysterious, powerful, yet sometimes shy animal at the centre of who you are. This means putting boundaries in terms of how we speak (v. 24), what we give as attention to our eyes (v. 25) and where we go (vv. 26–27). But it may also mean respecting our heart, and taking the time and energy to tend it. 'It is the wellspring of life' (v. 23, NIV 1984), whose life-giving flow cannot be taken for granted, but must, like any spring, be maintained and invested in to ensure it continues to flow cleanly and strongly.

The contemplative life is very much at the heart of what guarding your heart is about. It is a way of life oriented around a deep respect for the mystery that is our heart: a way of life that guards our outer activity from being disconnected from the inner source of its life that is our heart.

2 The imperative of stillness

Like many, I'm sure, I have returned to this psalm so many times over the years – and have done so again and again in these turbulent days we seem to be living in. For the invitation (or is it injunction?) in verse 10 seems to deliberately arrest the reader in its radical faith in the presence of God that is peace in the context of turmoil and strife.

The psalm may well have been composed at a time of crisis, perhaps the siege of Jerusalem (vv. 4–5). However, its historical setting is not as critical as its message – the sovereignty and power of God over the crises we may experience. And these crises include those of the natural world (vv. 1–3), city and societal life (vv. 4–5) and global conflict (vv. 6, 8–9). Such crises are still very much with us in this age of climate change, urban injustice and inequality, and troubling shifts in our geopolitics alongside numerous intractable conflicts.

But amidst these troubles, the God of life and peace is present. He is an ever-present help (or 'very present' – that is, near, suggesting a willingness to be found; v. 1). Like the 'wellspring of life' in yesterday's reading, God's life is once again described in terms of flowing water. It is because of this stream of God's presence that the besieged city will not fall (vv. 4–5). And these two ideas appear to come together in the imperative of verse 10, 'Be still, and know that I am God.'

We have become accustomed, perhaps, to hearing this verse as a gentle invitation from a genial God to come aside him, become quiet and tune into his presence. But the sense of the verse is primarily one of command, even rebuke. It may be a rebuke to the forces of nature, conflict and war (compare Mark 4:39). But it is also a command to come before God in stillness and acknowledge with awe his sovereignty over all the things. 'Be still!' is here more about disturbing us out of faithless anxiety than inviting us into comfort.

This raises the stakes on the value of contemplation. It is not just one invitation in our world of many choices, including spiritual ones. It is a command on those who serve the sovereign Lord, to be still in the face of the crises and troubles of our world, to know him (which in Hebrew always has a sense of relationship rather than simply information) and acknowledge him as Lord over all.

3 Contemplation and relinquishment

Ezekiel 37:1–6

Once again, the context of today's passage is crisis: the destruction of Jerusalem and the exile of most of its population to Babylon. A young priest was among the first wave of exiles and is called to be a prophet, in an extraordinary theophany at Babylon (Ezekiel 1—3). That man is Ezekiel. His ministry stands in the tension between priest and prophet, called upon to offer leadership while communicating an often-unpopular message of both judgement and hope. I see in Ezekiel a model of prophetic leadership in a time of crisis and renewal. And the journey of the prophecy of chapter 37 also outlines the spirituality needed to lead contemplatively in this context.

First, there is the confrontation with the reality of the situation. Ezekiel, already fully aware of it, from seeing the second wave of exiles come from Jerusalem with stories of horror and death, is nevertheless paraded up and down the valley of dry bones. He must be under no illusion that the power of Israel in the form of an empire and an army has gone (vv. 1–2).

So where does the way forward begin? It begins in knowing when you have nothing more to offer. 'Son of Man, can these bones live?' asks God (v. 3) – to which the answer might be an obvious 'no'. But the answer from Ezekiel is a stunning, 'Lord, you alone know.' Contemplation invites an attitude of unknowing, often a wordless surrendering, or relinquishment, of all our pretence of knowledge and therefore a posture of openness to the revelatory knowledge of God.

The contemplative life is closely aligned with the discipline of acknowledging the limits of our knowledge and agency. So much of our ministry, particularly when under pressure, becomes enterprise. It becomes the sum of our ideas and our energy and our resources and our haste. But ministry with God is the aligning of our agency with his, which always comes first. He initiates; we join in. To discipline ourselves away from enterprise and towards participation involves the practice of relinquishment – 'Lord, you alone know.'

What might this mean practically? Perhaps it is the practice of stillness before God with no agenda, no list. Perhaps it is the practice of breathing deeply, listening intently, pausing sufficiently in the face of apparent pressure to make a decision or do something. More than anything, it is an attitude, of relinquishing our assumptions, our agency, in order that the agency of God might be fully attended to and participated in.

4 A ministry with boundaries

As we explored on the first day this week, the principle of boundaries is a way of 'guarding our heart'. Here, that principle is expressed in the ministry of Jesus.

The context of this story is that of a tough period of ministry. Jesus' cousin John had been executed (14:1–11) and he seeks to withdraw to attend to his own grief (14:13). Yet the physical needs of the crowds that follow him (14:14–21) and his personal concern for his disciples (14:22–33) interrupt his own pursuit of solitude and rest. And there is pressure from the institution, too: a deposition from Jerusalem asking questions, seeking to unsettle him and those listening to his teaching (15:1–20).

Perhaps as a last resort, Jesus leaves Israel altogether and retreats to the area of Tyre and Sidon. His commitment to the solitude and rest he needs to restore his heart and soul is extraordinary. Yet even there, this commitment is tested when a Gentile woman comes seeking healing for her daughter.

This is a difficult passage. The blunt reading of the test makes Jesus look uncaring and even racist. Yet as one commentator suggests, there may be something of a 'twinkle in the eye' in Jesus' conversation with this woman. A similar somewhat jocular exchange is perhaps that between Jesus and the Samaritan woman of John 4.

But putting the racial theme to one side for a moment, the striking thing about Jesus' response for our purposes is his clear sense of the boundaries to his ministry. The boundary he sets here is a consequence of the limitations both of human need and of God's call on his life. Initially, he does not even answer the woman, so conscious is he of his own human need for rest (v. 23). His statement in verse 24 clearly articulates his deep sense of the limitations that his Father has placed on his ministry. It also suggests a deep trust in the wider salvation plan for the world of which his ministry is a part.

The boundaries of Jesus' ministry are porous, however. There is grace and a willingness to compromise (vv. 27–28). Nevertheless, the principle is there. Even Jesus practised a ministry with boundaries in order to guard his heart, his soul and his body from the pressures of ministry and to ensure that first and foremost in his life was his relationship with his heavenly Father.

5 Training (not trying) to grow in Christ

Philippians 3:12–21

Cultivating an attitude is not an easy thing. Attitudes mediate the expressions of much deeper states of our being. Changing our attitude takes time; we are seeking to rewire our hearts, minds and souls into a different posture, a different way of relating to the world and others. This is ultimately a work of Christ through the power of the Holy Spirit. However, it is a work we can participate in through our conscious effort.

In this passage from Paul's letter to the Philippians, we see something of the enormous effort to which Paul went to rewire his own soul towards 'that for which Christ Jesus took hold of me' (v. 12). For Paul, this is a committed, forward-facing determination to reach a goal which lies ahead of him (vv. 13–14). Interestingly, this goal is not what you might imagine, such as the planting of new Christian communities as far as Spain (something we know he also had an ambition to do; Romans 15:24), but the fulfilment of a relationship with Christ in the kingdom of heaven (vv. 14, 20).

Paul, for whom earthly ministry took up so much of his energy and attention, nevertheless saw his goal to keep his mind not 'on earthly things' but on the 'citizenship... in heaven' that awaited him (vv. 19–20). This must surely be a sobering reflection for many of us caught up in the busyness of our earthly lives. And for those in church ministry of some description, it is a powerful challenge to our priorities.

How, then, do we keep our relationship with Christ as our first priority, as that which we 'strain towards' in the midst of everyday life? Perhaps the metaphor that Paul employs helps. It is the metaphor of an athlete, running a race, reaching for the finishing line. As any athlete will know, behind any successful race lies a regime of months or even years of training: discipline, routines and practices, which slowly but consistently change someone from couch potato to proficient athlete, perhaps even to prize-winning runner.

It is no different in the life of a disciple. To seek after Christ in the midst of our relentlessly busy and noisy world, we must train our souls through disciplined practices – silence, stillness and sabbath, for example. These are fundamental in making space in which we may be with Jesus, space in which we may dwell in his presence. Is this a gospel of works? Or purely human effort? No, this is training, not trying. It is practically participating in a lifelong relationship with Jesus, which will be brought to its fulfilment, the transformation of our bodies, when we meet Christ in the kingdom of heaven (vv. 20–21).

6 A contemplative posture towards the world

Acts 17:16–34

While cultivating contemplation will involve practices, disciplines of stillness, silence and sabbath, for example, this is not the heart of what contemplation is. Contemplation is a lived posture, in the midst of the world, which is alert and open to the presence and action of God. Contemplation is therefore primarily a state of spiritual awareness, before it is any kind of practice, an openness to finding, listening and responding to God in the world.

Today's passage is a good example of what this lived posture looks like. Paul arrives in Athens with an agenda: he has a call to preach the gospel to the Gentiles with some urgency. And yet, while waiting for others to join him, he takes time to be present in the city (v. 16). As is his practice, he finds the local synagogue, but here engages in dialogue and debate, something that was very much part of Athenian culture (vv. 17–18, 21). Paul wanders the city, taking in the architecture and the iconography. And soon he is making connections with the gospel, connections that do not simply rubbish the idols or poetry of Athens, but that acknowledge something of the thirst for God that they express (vv. 24–28).

I do not believe this is simply an evangelistic marketing strategy, a way of coming alongside the Athenians in order to draw a receptive audience. The 'distress' (v. 16) that Paul feels towards the idolatry of Athens is not anger and judgement, but compassion borne out of a jealousy at the displacement of God from his place in the lives of the Athenian people. Without the contemplative posture of attentive listening to context, Paul would not have seen or valued the ways in which the idolatry of the Athenians also pointed to their desire for God.

Ironically it is Greek thought whose legacy in the west has been an unhealthy distinction between the sacred and the secular. Yet it is Athens where we see Paul demonstrating a contemplative posture towards the world, one where the presence of God, sometimes deeply hidden in the misplaced yearning of those he has created, enables us to listen, value and connect people to the fullness of this presence, made known in Jesus Christ.

Guidelines

We have travelled from the stillness of our hearts, to the limits of our capacities and vocation, and beyond that to the exercise of a contemplative posture in the world. It will take more than a week of Bible notes to cultivate an attitude of contemplation. Indeed, we will likely never cease in our exploration of the mysteries of God's presence in all of life.

We can continuously reflect on where we are and how we can deepen our awareness of God in the midst of life and ministry. Beginning at the foundations of contemplation, we might ask questions about our hearts and our will. Am I 'guarding my heart'? In what ways are we ensuring that the wellspring of our life in God is being attended to and protected? Are we obeying God's command to 'be still' – not simply as some kind of spiritual comfort, but as a practice of faith in an anxious world, and indeed an anxious church?

Both Ezekiel and Jesus demonstrated the importance of acknowledging the limitation to their abilities and ministry. Church ministers in particular can find themselves colluding with congregations and communities towards 'heroic' patterns of ministry and action which don't sufficiently value these limits. How could you be more honest about your own limitations? And what practices might embody a more realistic balance between your abilities and vocation and the grace and sovereignty of God?

Finally, Paul's life and ministry invite us to ask in what ways we continue to make our relationship with Christ a priority. It is so easy for the busyness and responsibility of ministry to take the place of our relationship with God. What practices are we integrating into our lives to ensure that we continue to 'take hold of that for which Christ Jesus took hold of me' (Philippians 3:12). And can we take the primacy of that relationship into our posture towards the world? Where do you see God at work in your community? Can your distress at the ignorance or dismissal of God become a step towards listening, engaging and finding connections for people between their lives and the fullness of life found in Jesus?

FURTHER READING

Paul Bradbury, *Stepping Into Grace: Moving beyond ambition to contemplative mission* (BRF, 2016).

Ian Cowley, *The Contemplative Minister: Learning to lead from the still centre* (BRF, 2015).

Thomas Merton, *New Seeds of Contemplation* (Shambhala, 2003).

Countercurrents in Joshua

Helen Paynter

Within the Christian canon, few books present as many challenges, or as difficult ones, as the book of Joshua. We (probably) like the book of Exodus, presented as God's saving work in bringing the people of Israel out of slavery in Egypt. We might struggle a bit with the death of the firstborn (a topic for another time!), but overall, we tend to view the narrative as one of liberation from oppression.

But after the exodus comes the story of the conquest – and this is another matter altogether, as the Israelites go on the offensive; they become the aggressors. Here, I anticipate that readers will fall into two camps. There will be those who have always been content with these stories, who (perhaps) learned them in Sunday school, and who (perhaps) preach and teach them today without any concerns about the validity of God's apparent command for the slaughter of thousands. And there will be others for whom these texts present a major challenge to their confidence in the goodness of God.

One for whom these texts are a problem is the Native American commentator Robert Warrior, who chillingly reminds us of the use of parts of Joshua by early European settlers in the New World. 'The obvious characters in the story for Native Americans to identify with are the Canaanites, the people who already lived in the promised land. As a member of the Osage Nation of American Indians, American Indians who stand in solidarity with other tribal people around the world, I read the Exodus stories with Canaanite eyes' (Robert Warrior, 'Canaanites, cowboys, and Indians', *Union Seminary Quarterly Review* 59 (2005), pp. 1–8).

It is not possible within the short space that we have here to examine the problem fully. Instead, we will pay attention to some helpful clues within the text of Joshua, which should give us pause. In a number of places, the narrative surprises us; one might even say it subverts itself. It seems to me that these 'countercurrents' are often overlooked. This set of readings is offered as an attempt to explore them.

Unless otherwise indicated, Bible quotations are from the ESV.

1 The boundaries of the land

Joshua 1

The new day has dawned. Moses is dead, and Joshua, previously always designated his assistant (e.g. Exodus 24:13), has assumed the mantle of leader. In this well-known chapter, the nascent leader is charged, commissioned and encouraged, first by God himself (vv. 2–9) and later by the people, who echo God's words (vv. 16–18). It is a passage simply made for preaching at ordinations or to muster the courage of the people of God: 'Be strong and courageous' (vv. 6, 9, 18). And it has been used this way on many occasions.

But in our pursuit of countercurrents, I'd like us to focus on something different. Take another look at verse 4. Here, in terms almost identical to those used in Deuteronomy 11:24, the promised land is laid out before Joshua in all its expansive scope. But if you care to get a map out, or if your geography is good enough without one, then you will see that this territory is simply enormous. Encompassing all of Jordan and Lebanon, most of Syria, half of Iraq, a good slice of Saudi Arabia, and part of Egypt, it utterly dwarfs the land ever actually owned by Israel.

It might be helpful to compare this territorial claim with some of the others in the Hebrew Bible. In Numbers 34:1–12, for example, much narrower borders are described for Israel, approximating the territory occupied by Israel today but with some extension into modern Syria and Jordan. In fact, there are, arguably, three or even four different descriptions of the territory of the promised land (see also Genesis 15:18–20; Ezekiel 47:17–18).

Those who study such matters have attempted to resolve this problem. The source critics (scholars who seek to identify the different source documents which have been compiled into the final form of the texts that we have today) claim that these are artefacts from the process of textual development. Others have sought to unify the different descriptions. But another possibility exists. This is that the vast, expansive land described in Joshua 1 is symbolic; it forms part of a rhetorical claim that is never realised, and was never intended to be realised, except in theological terms. Maybe this reflects the hope that the Abrahamic promise would one day reach the whole earth. The author of Psalm 2 (v. 8) and Isaiah 54 (v. 2) seem to agree.

2 The faith of Rahab

It's hard to render the choppy Hebrew of verses 6–8 into English. Normal word order would be verb-subject-object, although exceptions are permitted. Here we encounter a string of exceptions. *She* had taken them on to the roof… *the men* chased them… *the gate* they shut behind them… *they* had not yet lain down… *she* came up on to the roof to them. It fails to flow like normal Hebrew and therefore conveys a feeling of agitation.

This could, of course, relate to the excitement of the adventure. Will the spies be caught? Will the woman give them away? But there might be another reason for the agitation, or anticipation, and that lies in the astonishing words of Rahab which immediately follow: 'I know that the Lord has given you the land… for the Lord your God, he is God in the heavens above and on the earth beneath' (vv. 9, 11).

The Canaanites had plenty of their own deities. But Rahab calls upon the personal name of the God of the Israelites, declaring, 'YHWH your god, he is God!' In fact, not only is she laying a claim upon this foreign deity, but she is asserting his supremacy over the gods of her own family and clan.

There is more than that, though: she describes YHWH as being God 'in the heavens above and on the earth beneath'. Such language echoes the covenant language of, for example, Exodus 20:4 or Deuteronomy 5:8. As a statement of faith, it is only found in the mouths of two other individuals: the great Solomon (1 Kings 8:23) and the even greater Moses (Deuteronomy 4:39).

And there is one more thing that might be so daring as to agitate the narrator: the innocuous-sounding pair of words where Rahab reminds the spies that she has 'dealt kindly' with them and requests to being 'dealt kindly' in return and thus to be given a 'sure sign' of their trustworthiness (v. 12). The word rendered 'deal kindly' is the Hebrew word ḥesed, and 'sure' is 'emet. These are the primary words used to describe the character of God throughout the Old Testament: steadfast in love and faithful. (See, for example, Exodus 34:6.) This pagan woman, a prostitute no less, has a staggering apprehension of the character and covenant of God.

3 The man with the drawn sword

It is the eve of battle, and Joshua seems nervous. Like many battle commanders since, he paces out his worries by night – or at least, that is how I imagine it; the narrator is less specific. What the text is clear about is that Joshua meets a stranger, a man with a drawn sword, a description used elsewhere in the Old Testament for a warrior-angel (Numbers 22:23, 31; 1 Chronicles 21:16). Joshua is unnerved and offers him the traditional challenge, 'Friend or foe?' I think modern readers are insufficiently shocked by the answer that he receives.

Joshua does not know at this point that he is addressing the angel of the Lord. This only becomes apparent when the man identifies himself as the commander of the armies of the Lord. If Joshua had known, I don't believe he would have asked the question, for it would have seemed somewhat redundant. Thus far in his life, and in the story of Israel, Joshua has never really had any cause to doubt that God is entirely on Israel's side. Joshua is one of the generation that came out of Egypt. He witnessed the mighty works of God in delivering the Hebrews from slavery: the plagues, the death of the firstborn, the parting of the Red Sea. He stood, along with the rest of the people, at the foot of Mount Sinai as it shook and smoked and God made covenant with the nation of Israel and declared, 'You shall be my treasured possession among all peoples' (Exodus 19:5). Joshua was one of those fed in the desert with manna and quails; he was part of the generation that defeated Arad and Og in the desert (Numbers 21). True, they had suffered military losses to Amalek (Numbers 14), but that was through their own direct disobedience.

But Joshua does not know whom he is speaking with, and so he asks the question, 'Are you for us, or for our adversaries?' (v. 13); and the reply comes back, 'No.' If Joshua was unnerved before, he should be more so now. This angel that commands the host of heaven is not on Joshua's side. True, the Israelites will go on to win the forthcoming battle (but will lose the next). But God is not, wholly and unconditionally, on their side. Here, in the story about Joshua's conquests, we catch a glimpse of something bigger than Joshua has known. God has greater concerns and his loving gaze encompasses more than one nation.

This countercurrent should condition our reading of the whole of the remainder of the book of Joshua.

4 Rahab and the red cord

Joshua 6:6–27

If the story of the battle of Jericho is much-loved by Sunday-school teachers seeking to engage kinaesthetic learners (how many of us who grew up in church did not march around a 'city' of cardboard boxes, blowing on paper shofars?), then the story of Rahab is only a little less popular. Rahab, the prostitute, who finds herself in the family tree of Jesus (Matthew 1:5). Rahab, woman of faith, who hid the spies and was rewarded with life when the rest of her city died.

Various writers have discussed the red cord which she hangs out of her window to identify her house to the army (2:18, 21). Some writers have linked it to the red cord tied around the wrist of Zerah in Genesis 38:28, 30. Certainly Zerah gets a surprising mention in Matthew's genealogy, though it is unclear what the significance of this might be. Typological interpretation links Rahab's red cord to the blood of Christ. My hunch is that this is ultimately correct, but by less direct means than typology.

It might help if we pause to visualise the scene. Once the battle proper starts, Joshua's army will be attacking Jericho through any gate, door or window that they can access. They will, after all, be completely surrounding the city. So the most direct route into Rahab's house is through her window. This is why the cord is hanging here, rather than over the doorway into the streets of the city.

Notice the spies' instructions to her in 2:18–19: 'Gather into your house your father and mother, your brothers, and all your father's household. Then if anyone goes out of the doors of your house into the street, his blood shall be on his own head.' Compare this with the instructions given by Moses to the people of Israel on the night of the death of the firstborn. Each household was to gather at home, to eat in haste and be ready to depart, with the blood of the lamb painted on their doorframes. And they were warned, 'None of you shall go out of the door of his house until the morning... the Lord will pass over the door and will not allow the destroyer to enter your houses to strike you' (Exodus 12:22–23).

In both instances, the marker – to indicate to the destroyer that those sheltering inside are to be kept safe – consists of red streaks around the entranceway. The story of Rahab is looking very much like a Passover for this Canaanite.

5 Achan and Rahab

Rahab, the pagan prostitute, has seized hold of the opportunity presented to her by the coming of the spies: calling upon God by his personal name, laying claim to his character and invoking covenant language. Her faith has been rewarded with an astonishing rescue that mirrors the Passover event which saw Israel delivered from Egypt. We should remember that the deliverance of Israel by God was the defining moment in making Israel his people (Exodus 19:4–6).

After the rescue, Rahab is brought 'outside the camp of Israel' (6:23). This was consistent with the standard treatment of things or people who are unclean. But only two verses later we learn that she has been moved: 'She has lived in Israel to this day.' Translating the Hebrew word *qereb* with 'in', as here in the ESV, or as 'among' (NIV), rather misses the intensity of this word. At root, it refers to the entrails of an animal, its 'innards'. So the NASB says, 'She has lived in the midst of Israel to this day'; or one might try 'in the heart of Israel'.

We meet *qereb* again in chapter 7, where, after the disastrous attack upon Ai, God tells Joshua that something designated *ḥerem* is 'in your midst' (vv. 12–13). The *ḥerem*, or ban, was the order to consecrate everything to God; people and things could be designated *ḥerem* and thus were subject to the ban. For people, this often meant death, as here in the Jericho story. So when the reader sees these words, 'something *ḥerem* is in your midst', it might be natural to assume that God is speaking about Rahab, who was subject to the *ḥerem*, and has been brought, living, into the heart of the camp.

However, it is not Rahab whose presence in the heart of the nation is causing offence, but the spoil that Achan has taken for himself (vv. 1, 11). The outrage of this unlawful thing being brought into the very heart of the nation is intensified for us by the drawing of lots; our gaze zooms inward and inward as the noose tightens around Achan. And the goods are found in the middle (a different Hebrew word) of his tent (vv. 21, 23).

But there is yet another twist. By stealing it, Achan the Israelite has himself become *ḥerem* (6:18; v. 12). And so his journey is the exact opposite of Rahab the Canaanite's: out of the heart of the nation, to death.

6 The covenant renewal

It is time for Joshua and the people to renew the covenant with God. They gather at Mount Ebal, prescribed in Deuteronomy 11:29 and 27:4–14 as the place the people were to gather to renew the covenant after they had entered the land. Our narrator has taken pains to demonstrate how closely Joshua follows Moses' instructions; interestingly his actions in copying out the law (v. 32) are similar to the law for the accession of a king (Deuteronomy 17:18).

Two different types of sacrifice are offered: burnt offerings and fellowship (or peace) offerings (v. 31). Burnt offerings were entirely consumed, and were offered for sin (see Leviticus 1:4). Fellowship offerings were eaten in the presence of the Lord and were much more like a festival (Leviticus 7:11–17), focusing on the relationship with God and with others in the community.

Next, the people line themselves up in what must have been the most spectacular piece of theatre. Half of the nation are on the slopes of Mount Ebal and half on Mount Gerizim. According to the instructions in Deuteronomy, the covenant curses were to be proclaimed on Mount Ebal, and the blessings on Mount Gerizim, opposite. We are to imagine a grand antiphonal recitation between the two halves of the nation. And then Joshua reads the law to the people.

So we have these elements, all generally held to be particular to the nation of Israel: covenant, fellowship/community, atonement, law. It would therefore be more than reasonable to assume that this great ceremony would involve the men only. After all, it is only men who bear in their flesh the mark of the covenant. It would also be reasonable to imagine that it would only include the adults. The pragmatic challenge of keeping small children contained and engaged during prolonged services of worship will be familiar to many readers. And we could be pretty certain that it would only be true-blooded Israelites who could participate. At the making of the covenant at Sinai, did God not say, 'If you will indeed obey my voice and keep my covenant, you shall be my treasured possession among all peoples' (Exodus 19:5)?

But we are told who is present (vv. 33, 35), and if we have paid attention in Deuteronomy we will know that this, too, was commanded: men, women, little ones and resident aliens. Yes, non-Israelites were included in this great covenant renewal. Inclusion of the resident alien within the cultic festivals is a theme that often recurs (Exodus 12:43–49; 20:10; Deuteronomy 16:10–14; 26:10–11), but it is one we frequently miss.

Guidelines

In the creation mandate (Genesis 1:28), which is reiterated to Noah at the flood (Genesis 9:1), the language of spreading out and filling the earth conveys the idea of taking God's glory to the ends of the earth. In Genesis 12:1–3, when God calls Abram, his purpose of blessing beyond the Abrahamic blood line is clear. So in God's relationship with Israel, there is both particularity ('You shall be my treasured possession among all peoples', Exodus 19:5) and universality. These dual themes are reflected later in the prophets ('You only have I known of all the families of the earth', Amos 3:2; 'It shall come to pass in the latter days that the mountain of the house of the Lord shall be established as the highest of the mountains, and shall be lifted up above the hills; and all the nations shall flow to it, and many peoples shall come, and say: "Come, let us go up to the mountain of the Lord, to the house of the God of Jacob, that he may teach us his ways and that we may walk in his paths"', Isaiah 2:2–3).

In this week's readings, we have seen a pagan woman who lays claim to the name and character of God being brought into the heart of the nation; the divine assertion that God is not wholly on Israel's side during the conquest; and the inclusion of resident aliens at the covenant renewal. And all of this is prefaced by the hint in chapter 1 that the borders of the nation are universal. In this book, which is traditionally held to be particularising and militaristic, these are strong, and surprising, countercurrents.

1 The Gibeonites

Joshua 9

I think the standard way to teach or preach on this story is to criticise Joshua and the elders of Israel for failing to enquire of the Lord (v. 14) before making a binding agreement with the Gibeonites. But there is a countercurrent in this wonderful story of ancient trickery which is much stronger than the rebuke of Joshua.

Gibeah was probably where modern Al Jib stands, about eight miles from Jerusalem, and therefore right within the midst (*qereb*, vv. 7, 16, 22) of Israelite territory. Also known as the Hivites, the Gibeonites were one of the people groups subject to the ḥerem order (Deuteronomy 7:1–2). Here, they have heard of the sweeping conquest of Joshua and make an extraordinary decision. Rather than fleeing or fighting, as other people groups were doing, they travel headlong to meet their fate: 'Your servants have come, because of the name of the Lord your God' (v. 9). Like Rahab, they too call upon the God of the Israelites by his personal name, and refer to his mighty deeds (vv. 9–10). In fact, pagans often seem to find it easier to trust God on the basis of his miraculous actions than the Israelites do (Numbers 13:25–33).

As a result of their elaborate ruse, Joshua makes a treaty with the Gibeonites, called by its standard name: a *berit*, a covenant. Covenants like this were made between nations or people groups quite often (for example, see Genesis 21:22–34; 1 Kings 5). But the frequency with which the word is used here (vv. 6–7, 11, 15–16) suggests that the narrator wishes to foreground it; we should, perhaps, have another, larger, covenant in view. If this is the case, then what the Gibeonites are doing is somehow seizing hold of the blessings of the covenant for themselves. By making a covenant with Israel, they have indirectly made a covenant with God.

And this accidental peace (*shalom*, v. 15) which Joshua consents to is successful. The Gibeonites are permitted to live in the heart of the nation. They are given jobs to do – admittedly menial ones, but hewers of wood and drawers of water will never be out of work in the ancient world. In fact, they are permitted to work at the sanctuary itself (v. 27). Indeed, their embeddedness becomes more and more apparent as the biblical storyline unfolds. In the next chapter, Joshua calls out the fighting men of Israel in their defence; by the time of Nehemiah, Gibeonites play a key role in rebuilding the walls of Jerusalem (Nehemiah 3:7).

2 Sweeping all before him?

Joshua 10:16–43; 11:21–23

As someone who specialises in the interpretation of biblical violence, and as director of the Centre for the Study of Bible and Violence, I'm often asked about the conquest of Canaan. Why does a good God command the slaughter of the Canaanites? Last year, when I spoke in multiple venues around the country, on a different but related theme, I was asked this question afterwards *every single time*. It's one of the most difficult questions that the church in this country is facing, in my opinion, because of the pastoral and missional implications that it has. People are losing their faith because of it.

People who ask this very reasonable question generally have the view that Joshua and his warriors scorched into the land killing everyone in their wake. Indeed, this is the way that the story is usually told, in churches, in Sunday schools and in conversation. But in actual fact, the situation is far more ambiguous than this, as the text itself tells us.

Take a look at Joshua 10:20. In the first half of the verse we read, 'When Joshua and the sons of Israel had finished striking them with a great blow until they were wiped out', which would lead us to believe that everyone was slaughtered. But without drawing breath, our narrator tells us, 'and when the remnant that remained of them had entered into the fortified cities...' There is a clear tension between the two descriptions. Or compare Joshua 10:38–39, 'Joshua and all Israel... captured [Debir] with its king and all its towns. And they struck them with the edge of the sword and devoted to destruction every person in it; he left none remaining,' with 11:21, 'Joshua came at that time and cut off the Anakim from the hill country... from Debir.' The account in chapter 10, that there were no survivors in Debir, appears to be contradicted by the record that he returned later to attack the survivors in the city.

There are other examples, too. Compare Joshua 11:21–22 with 15:14; Judges 1:8 with Judges 1:21; and Joshua 11:23 with Judges 2:21–23. The presence of variant voices like this within the text (whether penned by the same hand or not) is termed 'polyphony'. It has been described in many parts of the Old Testament, and here we have a good example. Polyphony is a way of exploring truth, of testing and probing and debating what is not clear-cut.

The issue of the conquest of Canaan is complex and disturbing, but noticing the text's own ambivalence might be the first step to helping us to work out our own stance towards the issue.

3 Seeking peace with Israel

This is one of those troublesome passages that appear to show Joshua massacring the entire population of Canaan. In addition to yesterday's comment, there are a few further remarks to make and then two small countercurrents to note.

First, we should note the rhetorical, stylised nature of the language. If we take this entirely at face value, Joshua behaved exactly the same way ('he struck it with the edge of the sword') in every city that he took. In fact, the language is highly stylised and repetitious, suggesting that there is more to this than a bald statement of battle casualties. In addition there is, in the wider text, frequent use of the motif of 'seven', which should alert us that rhetorical devices are at work. This account is consistent with the hyperbolic way that all ancient Near-Eastern warriors recorded their victories. It is routine to describe the conquest as a massacre.

Second, we should not be too quick to assume that we understand exactly what was meant by the word ḥerem. Depending on your translation, it has probably been rendered 'devote to destruction' (ESV), 'put to death' (GNT) or 'totally destroy' (NIV). But to equate ḥerem with death is too simplistic. Clearly it sometimes, perhaps often, involved death. But not always. People who were ḥerem could be redeemed from death, for example, as Rahab and the Gibeonites were. Items could also be designated ḥerem, and may not even be destroyed (e.g. Numbers 18:14). At root, the word means 'set apart for God'.

Third, pragmatically, people do not sit around waiting to be destroyed. The towns Joshua attacked probably only contained fighting men by the time he got there.

And finally, there are two small countercurrents in this chapter. The first is in the hamstringing of horses (v. 9). Horses and chariots were the ancient world's equivalent of cruise missiles; they were elite military equipment. Israel did not have them, and the Canaanites did. In this text, at least, the actions of Israel are characterised as those of an oppressed peasant minority destroying the military technology of a superior force.

The second countercurrent is found in the surprising reference to the nations being destroyed because they did not sue for peace as the Hivites (Gibeonites) had (v. 19). There was no provision for making terms of peace in the instructions handed down from Moses. But here there is a hint that it might have been possible. If it was possible for the Gibeonites, why not for the other nations?

4 Caleb's daughter

Joshua 15:1–18

Sadly, the offering of a woman to incentivise male warriors is not unique to today's passage. Saul also does it, which is how David acquires Michal as wife (1 Samuel 18:20–25). Here, Caleb's younger brother Othniel, who will later become a judge in Israel (Judges 3:9–11), acquires his niece Achsah as a prize for conquering Kiriath-sepher.

Of course, this is distasteful to us as modern readers, but we must recall that the narrator has not commented upon the transaction for good or ill. He simply records that it happened. We are left to wonder what Achsah thought of the matter; our ancient narrator probably never even considered this.

This makes the next part of the little drama more surprising. Although women are often silenced in biblical texts, Achsah proves to be irrepressible. She is the driving force that persuades her husband to ask her father for territory. Why does she then appear to approach Caleb herself? Maybe because her husband has not managed to negotiate the water source that they need in that arid country. Maybe she becomes impatient and takes matters into her own hands. Maybe she simply has to gain her husband's consent before asking Caleb herself.

The telling of history is always a selective enterprise, by nature of our being finite people. The nature of biblical history is less disinterested than the more objective forms of modern historiography, because our narrator has a strong theological purpose. So asking why a certain narrative has been included is always a fruitful question, because it was not incorporated by accident. Here, our narrator is probably solidifying Caleb's claim to certain territory. And in order to do this, he is giving voice to a feisty woman, who makes her own claim. Somewhat like Rahab before her, this young woman sees the chance to benefit from the promise the God has given his people, and she capitalises upon it.

5 The daughters of Zelophehad

Joshua 16:1—17:6

Here, we read of the all-important allocation of what will henceforth be the ancestral land of the tribes, clans and families of Israel. Ancestral land was extremely important to the people of Israel. There were careful laws to ensure that, if it had to be sold through extreme poverty, it should be redeemed as soon as possible. In any case at the jubilee it would be returned to the family (Leviticus 25:23–28). Historians tell us that an individual's property was not regarded as belonging solely to him, but to his family past and future; the current incumbent was under obligation to both his ancestors and to his descendants to preserve and protect the land. It is this sense of obligation which caused Naboth to refuse to sell his vineyard to King Ahab (1 Kings 21:3).

For a man, having sons was a vital element to a fulfilled life. A son would continue to live in the ancestral land, and he would perpetuate the father's memory. This set of ideas is summarised as 'having a name in the land'. Hence Bildad speaks of the wicked man in Job 18:17, 'His memory perishes from the earth, and he has no name in the street', and Isaiah offers the blessing in 66:22, 'so shall your offspring and your name remain'.

For Zelophehad, father of five daughters and no sons, his early demise before this allocation of territory was a catastrophe in these terms. In Numbers 27:1–11, we read of the daughters approaching Moses and requesting an inheritance along with the menfolk, saying, 'Why should the name of our father be taken away from his clan because he had no son?' In response, Moses consulted the Lord and ruled that they could indeed receive an inheritance in their own right. Indeed, this case became legal precedent that put daughters into the line of succession after sons but before brothers (Numbers 27:8–11).

In Joshua 17:4, these same women step forward to stake their claim. It is unclear whether this was simply standard procedure or whether they were in danger of being overlooked in the allocation. There would surely have been vested family interests which would have cheerfully 'forgotten' the women's entitlement. And so they plead their case all over again. They have already made it to Moses; now they make it again to Joshua. Interestingly, on this occasion they make no mention of perpetuating their father's name, but simply assert their own entitlement.

In reward, they are granted five allotments, not a single one divided between the five of them. And the narrator has carefully preserved not only their father's name, but their own.

6 'You are not able to serve the Lord'

Joshua 24:1–28

In the ancient Near East, of which the nation of Israel was a part, treaties were frequently made between warring parties, or between an overlord and his vassal. Such treaties, or covenants, were inscribed on clay or stone for posterity. We have found some of these: the Mesopotamian Stele of the Vultures, currently housed in the Louvre, and the Egyptian-Hittite Treaty of Kadesh, now displayed in Istanbul and Berlin. These treaties tended to follow a standard pattern: preamble, historical prologue, stipulations, provision for the record to be permanently stored (the so-called 'tablet clause'), witnesses, curses and blessings.

Such treaties bear significant points of similarity with many of the biblical covenants. (See, for example, the extended list of covenant blessings and curses in Deuteronomy 28.) We find most of these features in this covenant renewal which Joshua institutes. Verse 2 forms the preamble, and the antecedent history is reviewed in verses 2–13. The tablet clause is in verses 25–27, and the witnesses, curses and blessings are found in 19–24. Within the second half of the account, the theme word (Leitwort) is *'abad*, serve. I count ten instances between verses 14 and 24.

Within this context, Joshua's words in verses 19–20 are surprising. 'Serve the Lord,' he has urged the people in verse 14. But when the people affirm that they will, Joshua then tells them they can't: 'You are not able to serve the Lord, for he is a holy God. He is a jealous God; he will not forgive your transgressions or your sins. If you forsake the Lord and serve foreign gods, then he will turn and do you harm and consume you, after having done you good.'

There is a significant countercurrent here at the close of the book of Joshua. Serve, but you are not able to serve. You must, but you can't. We need not be disconcerted about this, however. Sensitive reading of the Old Testament will frequently reveal such tensions. Here, the combination of invitation and warning reflects the Torah's testimony, particularly in the book of Exodus, concerning the divine presence. The presence of God is both utterly desirable – see Exodus 3:12; 33:15 – but at the same time utterly terrifying and liable to be consuming – Exodus 3:4–6; 33:3, 20.

Israel, the nation with whom God has chosen to make covenant, is summoned to serve and worship God, and at the very same moment, the impossibility of that charge is asserted. It will be many centuries before that problem is resolved.

Guidelines

In the readings this week, we have seen further examples of the counter-current that we focused on last week, particularly in the inclusion of the Gibeonites. This provides more evidence that the ethnic boundaries of Israel were quite porous – an assertion that could be supported by reference to many other parts of the Old Testament, too. Position in the nation relates to faith and obedience, and can be lost as well as gained. In an age when ethnic distinctions are once again coming to the fore in many parts of Europe, it is vital that we understand that the Old Testament does not provide justification for such a polemic.

The two narratives about women might likewise surprise us. In a deeply patriarchal society, not only do these women receive an allocation of land alongside the men, but the narrator has bothered to tell us about it. Women will have an even more striking role in the book of Judges, which follows.

Both of these themes are developed far more clearly in the ministry of Jesus and then of the early church: 'I have other sheep that are not of this fold' (John 10:16); 'There is neither Jew nor Greek, there is neither slave nor free, there is no male and female, for you are all one in Christ Jesus' (Galatians 3:28). But they are present here, in the earliest days of the establishment of the nation of Israel.

FURTHER READING

Walter Brueggemann, *Divine Presence amid Violence: Contextualising the book of Joshua* (Cascade, 2009).

Paul Copan and Matthew Flannagan, *Did God Really Command Genocide? Coming to terms with the justice of God* (Baker, 2014).

Yohanna Katanacho, *The Land of Christ: A Palestinian cry* (Pickwick, 2013).

Helen Paynter, *God of Violence Yesterday, God of Love Today? Wresting honestly with the Old Testament* (BRF, 2019).

John H. Walton and J. Harvey Walton, *The Lost World of the Israelite Conquest: Covenant, retribution and the fate of the Canaanites* (IVP, 2017).

The established church

Graham Dow

This is a most unusual assignment: to write some Bible studies on 'the established church'. Presumably, it was believed that as a bishop in the established Church of England, I will have given some thought to this. Well, now I have!

The church may be said to be established when the constitutions of the nation give to that church legally binding designated authority and roles. This happens when the nation's leaders believe that the worship of God and recognition of his ultimate authority are essential for the nation's well-being and good governance.

The Church of England was established as the church of the nation by the Act of Supremacy in 1534, with the sovereign as the head of the church. Parliament has subsequently dissolved the established church in Wales and Ireland. The established church in Scotland is the Presbyterian Church.

Since the Act of Settlement in 1701, our sovereign has been required to join in Communion in the Church of England. This has barred from the monarchy those who adhere to other Christian faith traditions or none. It has affected the choice of consorts by potential monarchs.

At the coronation of our present Queen Elizabeth, she received from the Archbishop of Canterbury the orb set under the cross. The archbishop said, 'Remember that the whole world is subject to the power and empire of Christ our redeemer'. She received the sceptre with the words 'Receive the rod of equity and mercy'. This symbol of justice and mercy, given by the church's representative, is a statement of what God expects in good government.

The state appoints senior Church of England leaders: bishops, most cathedral deans and some others. The process for diocesan bishops has been refined over the years. Following the choice of two bishops ranked in order of preference by the church, the prime minister presents a recommendation to the Queen. It is well known that on occasions the PM has selected the second name.

In these studies, we consider the relationship between Christ's kingdom, the church and the state; the positives and dangers of an established church; and whether establishment inevitably compromises the prophetic witness of the church to the kingdom of God. How is the goal of the kingdom of God best sought in a nation? Only in the Old Testament do we find a partnership in faith between the people of God and the government.

Unless otherwise stated, Bible quotations are taken from the NRSV.

1 The kingdom, the church and the state

John 18:33–38; 19:8–12

The goal for the world is that God's kingdom shall come, his will be done on earth. Jesus announced that the kingdom of God was breaking in with his coming.

Jesus declares to Pilate, 'My kingdom is not from this world' (v. 36). His kingdom is of a spiritual reality from heaven, revealing truth to the world. Pilate mockingly says, 'What is truth?' (v. 38). The truth includes the reality that God has power over all human institutions. The only power Pilate has over Jesus is the power given to him by God.

Jesus says, 'I will build my church, and the gates of Hades will not prevail against it' (Matthew 16:18). His final instructions to his apostles are to make disciples of all the nations, teaching them to observe everything he had commanded the twelve (Matthew 28:19–20). The united fellowship of Jesus' disciples, under the power of the Holy Spirit, prophetically seeks to affect change in earthly society.

If you use the word 'political' to refer to a new state of affairs in which people give their ultimate and wholehearted allegiance to someone other than Caesar – and if you call 'political' the establishment of cells of people loyal to their new ruler, celebrating his rescuing rule and living in new kinds of communities as a result – then what Paul was doing was inescapably 'political'. It had to do with the foundation of a new polis, right at the heart of the existing system.

Tom Wright, *Paul: A biography* (SPCK, 2018), p. 106

The new ruler is Jesus and the polis (city) is the church. The vision of Jesus is a church that is one, a unity (John 17:21); it is the one body of Christ in the world (1 Corinthians 12:13). Such a body needs a strong framework of leadership if it is to bring change to society, a leadership which looks to God's authority. The church poses a threat to the state until the state embraces it. But has the state then become a threat to the integrity of the church?

The kingdom of God challenges all political systems. Both religious and secular leaders, guarding their own positions, want to get rid of the prophetic challenge to the way they do things. Christians are seriously persecuted in over 50 countries.

2 Political expediency and a heart for God

1 Samuel 8

Political expediency governs the decision of the people of Israel to ask Samuel to appoint a king.

Following the settlement in the promised land, God raises up charismatic leaders who deliver them from their enemies. He raises up Samuel as prophet and judge; his anointing is widely recognised in the nation. When Samuel grows old, he appoints his corrupt sons as judges. Seeing the success of the surrounding nations, the tribal leaders of Israel instead ask for a king to govern them. God sees this as a rejection of him, a continuation of the nation's disposition to forsake Yahweh and serve other gods (vv. 1–8)

God instructs Samuel to follow their request, but to warn them solemnly about how their king will treat them (v. 9). When they see how they are treated, they will cry out to God, but the Lord will not answer them (v. 18). Samuel anoints Saul as king (10:1), and a form of establishment begins since the king was the focus of the faith of the nation.

Political expediency led King Henry VIII to end the establishment of the church of Rome in England. Failing to get from the Pope the divorce from Catherine of Aragon, and desperate for a male heir, he invoked the divine right of kings anointed by God and declared the Church of England to be separate from the authority of the Pope. When diocesan bishops today have to swear the oath to the Queen and to recognise 'no other prelate', we know which prelate is in mind! Some bishops find this difficult.

How does the truth 'the Lord is king' get translated into earthly government? Scripture offers no one model. It appears that where leaders have a heart towards God, he will bless different forms of government. Samuel declares, 'If both you and the king who reigns over you will follow the Lord your God, it will be well; but if you will not heed the voice of the Lord, but rebel against the commandment of the Lord, then the hand of the Lord will be against both you and your king' (12:14–15). But he also warns, 'Only fear the Lord, and serve him faithfully with all your heart… But if you still do wickedly, you shall be swept away, both you and your king' (12:24–25).

3 Nation and faith in harmony

1 Chronicles 23:2–6, 24–32

The Spirit of the Lord comes mightily on King Saul (1 Samuel 10:6, 10–11). He saves the people from the Philistines. Then his test of obedience to Samuel's command comes very quickly, and the deeply insecure king takes matters into his own hands. Samuel rebukes Saul for his foolish behaviour. His kingdom will not continue; the Lord has sought out a man after his own heart and has appointed David to be ruler over his people (13:8–14).

At the end of David's reign, as immortalised by Handel, Zadok the priest and Nathan the prophet anoint Solomon king (1 Kings 1:34, 39). God's pleasure is expressed in 1 Chronicles 29:25: 'The Lord highly exalted Solomon in the sight of all Israel, and bestowed upon him such royal majesty as had not been on any king before him in Israel.' The time of the kings David and Solomon becomes an age of blessing and greatness.

How much authority should the state exercise over the worship of the people? David, we read in 1 Chronicles 23, organises the Levites to maintain all of the functions of the house of the Lord. Putting aside the fact that the Levitical author is reading back into David's reign the ceremonies of worship (and the books of Chronicles are the most high-church books in the Bible), we read that David assigns to the Levites the role of assisting the descendants of Aaron (the priests) in the service of the house of the Lord. They are to be responsible for the care of the building, the cleansing of all that is holy, the making of bread and grain offerings, and the singing of the Lord's praises daily.

The careful naming of the different Levitical houses (vv. 7–23) indicates the king's personal interest in the families and their assignments. The king acts on behalf of God: there is no disapproval of the king's role in appointing them; state and faith are completely integrated with a God-loving king. Since membership of both priesthood and Levitical order was by family descent, this was a useful check on royal power having the sole prerogative of appointment.

If the establishment of the church in the state amounts to making the church the official voice of prophecy in the nation, how compromised will it be? When a nation's faith recedes and churches are disestablished, is there greater freedom for religious differences and prophetic challenge?

4 Right attitudes and the potential for corruption

1 Kings 3:1–15

'Solomon loved the Lord, walking in the statutes of his father David' (v. 3). We see how good earthly kingship relates to the Lord as king. Solomon goes to Gibeon to sacrifice and the Lord appears to him in a dream, saying, 'Ask what I should give you' (v. 5). In his reply, Solomon remembers God's great love to his father David: 'I am only a little child; I do not know how to go out or come in' (v. 7). As God's servant, he asks for 'an understanding mind to govern your people, able to discern between good and evil; for who can govern this your great people?' (v. 9).

Solomon expresses exemplary attitudes. They resonate with Jesus saying we must become like children to enter the kingdom of God. God is pleased and promises Solomon a wise and discerning mind. But it is the nature of God to give many blessings to those who love and fear him, so Solomon is also promised riches and honour for which he had not asked. The ultimate kingship of God can work very well through rulers on earth with humble, God-fearing attitudes.

Just as Solomon was anointed, so, on the day of her coronation, Queen Elizabeth II was anointed on the palms of hands, her breasts and her head. She regarded that moment as a very personal moment between her and God; it was not allowed to be televised.

In British history, there has been plenty of collusion in the ungodly use of power between state and church. Long after its ascendancy, the Church of England, hand in hand with the state, persecuted Roman Catholics and Protestant dissenters. It was not until the Toleration Act of 1689 that legal existence was given to Protestant groups outside the Church of England, and the Roman Catholic Relief Act wasn't enacted until 1829. The fight for abolition of slavery was long and hard. Vested interests corrupt both parliament and church. Apartheid was for many years condoned by the Dutch

Reformed Church in South Africa. On a positive note, in the service following the Falklands War, and to the irritation of the British prime minister, Archbishop Runcie insisted on prayer for the Argentinians as well as the British. It is not the establishment of the church that is wrong; it is when the established church fails to hear and respond to God's prophetic voices.

5 The suffering of God's prophets

Jeremiah 20:1–7; 21:1–10

Pashhur is the chief officer in the house of the Lord (20:1). He belongs to the faith establishment. Offended by Jeremiah's prophecy of disaster, he throws the prophet into the stocks. Jeremiah replies prophetically that Pashhur and his household will go into captivity, along with his friends to whom he has prophesied falsely. The established church faces similar dangers: false prophecy used to protect vested interests and ignoring or taking reprisals against true prophecy.

The rest of chapter 20 is Jeremiah's powerful lament: so great is the fire of the Lord's word in his bones, and the cost of delivering it, that he says it would be better if he had not been born (vv. 9, 14–18). To be a prophet challenging government is a very painful place to be. That is why there is so little of it in God's church.

King Zedekiah sends Pashhur to Jeremiah to enquire of the Lord's direction when the nation is facing attacks from just outside the walls from Nebuchadnezzar, king of Babylon. Jeremiah answers saying that the Chaldeans will enter the city, killing many inhabitants. The city will be burnt. There will be no pity or compassion. Any hope of a miraculous deliverance by God (as in King Hezekiah's time) is folly. But the prophet offers the king a choice: the way of life and the way of death. Those who leave the city and surrender to the enemy will keep their lives (21:1–10).

Finally, God sends Jeremiah to speak directly to the king. If he will act with justice and righteousness, practise no wrong or violence and not shed innocent blood, God will give the monarchy a secure future. But if he will not heed these words, his house shall be a desolation (22:1–5). And so it was.

So how can the powerless prophet challenge a powerful king? Challenging David's adultery and his conspiracy to kill Uriah, Bathsheba's husband, the prophet Nathan told a story about a rich man who took a poor man's only lamb to feed his guests. 'David's anger was greatly kindled', but he was then told, 'You are the man!' (2 Samuel 12:1–15). David was truly convicted of sin, and tradition holds that he duly composed Psalm 51. For the powerless to appeal to the powerful, they must touch the conscience. The church, established or not, must learn this way.

6 Loyalty to both God and the state

Matthew 22:15–22

The Pharisees and the Herodians form an unholy alliance to get rid of Jesus. The question 'Is it lawful to pay taxes to the emperor, or not?' (v. 17) is a trick. If he says it is, he will lose the support of the crowds, who resent the Roman occupation of Israel. If he says it isn't, the Jewish leaders will take him straight to the Roman authorities as the leader of a rebellion.

Jesus points to the emperor's head on a denarius, money that everyone was using. He directs that Caesar be given what bears Caesar's image. On the other hand, he implies that as people created by God bear his image, so let God be given what bears God's image. With his simple distinction between loyalty to the state and to God, Jesus has avoided the trap. The intention to give ourselves to God and to do his will is not compromised by obedience to the rule of secular government. Since all earthly authority is given by God, believers can respect it.

Writing in AD57, the apostle Paul takes a similar line about Roman government in Romans 13:

Let every person be subject to the governing authorities; for there is no authority except from God, and those authorities that exist have been instituted by God… For rulers are not a terror to good conduct, but to bad… Then do what is good, and you will receive its approval; for it is God's servant for your good… It is the servant of God to execute wrath on the wrongdoer.

ROMANS 13:1, 3–4

Such is the light of God in all humanity (John 1:4–5, 9) that government which is not Christian can still promote good conduct.

However, where the state demands worship of its rulers, the biblical tradition supports refusal to obey (see Daniel 3 and 6). By the time of the book of Revelation, AD80 or later, the Roman Empire is seen as a demonic monster (Revelation 13). Christians are to remain faithful to Christ, even at risk of death.

Very sadly, in a similar situation in Nazi Germany, the established church largely colluded with Hitler instead of opposing his genocide.

Only in an extreme situation does the kingdom of Jesus support rebellion against state or church; but it judges all authority, and its followers must bide their time for victory.

Guidelines

Our studies suggest that God can promote his kingdom through state leadership when it acknowledges its dependence on God. A heart that is for God and for a rule of justice and mercy is what will promote the kingdom of God on earth. Establishment gives the church a prophetic platform in the nation from which it can speak and be heard. In my experience, the leaders of churches other than the Church of England are glad of that platform when Church of England leaders use it well. But, sadly, the church may collude with what is not righteous.

When positions of faith in a nation change, the time can come for total or partial disestablishment. In January 2000, the Church of Sweden ceased to have state support and Lutheranism ceased to be the country's official religion. In a more partial disestablishment, in 2012 the Norwegian constitution was revised to remove the Church of Norway as the official religion of the state.

Whether the church is established or not, we need to heed the apostle Paul's admonitions to pray for our rulers:

I urge that supplications, prayers, intercessions, and thanksgivings should be made for everyone, for kings and all who are in high positions, so that we may lead a quiet and peaceable life in all godliness and dignity. This is right and is acceptable in the sight of God our Saviour, who desires everyone to be saved and come to the knowledge of the truth.

1 TIMOTHY 2:1–4

Or, following 1 Timothy 2, as one Christian leader put it:

The first specific topic of prayer ordained by God for his people meeting in fellowship is the government. Extensive experience has convinced me that the vast majority of professing Christians never give any serious consideration to this topic in prayer.

Derek Prince, *Shaping History through Prayer and Fasting* (New Wine Press, 2008), p. 38

Do you consider that the established Church of England fulfils its God-given roles:

- in leading the nation's faith?
- in supporting and invoking God's blessing on the sovereign and the government?
- in prophetic challenge?

How could it fulfil these roles better?

FURTHER READING

Derek Prince, *Shaping History through Prayer and Fasting* (New Wine Ministries, 2008).

N.T. Wright, *How God Became King: The forgotten story of the gospels* (SPCK, 2012).

N.T. Wright, *Paul: A biography* (SPCK, 2018).

Philippians

Fiona Gregson

Paul's joy in partnership with and love for the Philippians is evident as he writes to them, to encourage them in face of his suffering and their suffering, to exhort them in unity, to reassure them about Epaphroditus and to strengthen their friendship and partnership in the gospel.

Philippi was an ancient town, named for Philip of Macedonia (356BC) and was the site of the defeat of Brutus and Cassius by Antony and Octavian in 42BC. It was then made a Roman colony with settlers of Roman soldiers.

The church in Philippi was founded by Paul, Silas and Timothy in AD48–49. Their visit was brief and ended following Paul and Silas' imprisonment and release. Living in a Roman colony would have presented particular difficulties to the Philippian believers, as there would have been expectations of worshipping the emperor as lord and saviour. We also see evidence in Paul's letter of ongoing challenges, including tensions within the church and suffering.

Paul (with Timothy) writes the letter to the Philippians some years later from prison. It is not clear which imprisonment Paul is writing from and there are arguments for Rome (early 60s), Caesarea (late 50s) or Ephesus (mid-50s). The last of these would more easily fit with the movement we see of messengers between Paul and the Philippians (Epaphroditus to Paul, message to Philippians about Epaphroditus' illness, message of concern from Philippians) and would account for his hope to be able to see them soon. After all, if Paul is in Rome in prison, we might expect him to go from there to Spain (Romans 15:23–24).

So as we look at Philippians (and the relevant Acts passages), may we also be encouraged in our discipleship – in partnership, in unity and in the face of suffering and uncertainty.

Unless otherwise stated, Bible quotations are from the TNIV.

1 When God says no...

As Paul, Silas and now Timothy travel on from Derbe and Lystra, twice they are prevented from continuing in the direction they intend: 'having been kept by the Holy Spirit' (v. 6) and then 'the Spirit of Jesus would not allow them' (v. 7). The text is sparse, and it is not clear exactly what it means that the Holy Spirit/Spirit of Jesus guided them – inner conviction, outward circumstances or prophetic utterance – nor whether they continued to preach along the route as they travelled. Eventually, after a journey of over 200 miles (at least two weeks), along which they seem only to be directed negatively by God, they arrive in Troas, where they finally receive some positive guidance with Paul having a dream or vision of a man from Macedonia. Not only are Paul and his companions led by double guiding – both prohibition and permission – to a new area for evangelism, but they are also led to a new possible pattern of mission.

The detail of Paul's ministry in Acts thus far has primarily centred on Paul and his companions preaching in a synagogue as a first port of call (13:5, 14; 14:1). This was only possible in places where there were sufficient (at least ten) Jewish men to form a synagogue and enabled an obvious inroad for evangelism, but it could also lead to conflict and danger (13:45; 14:19). It is possible that, as Paul and his companions sought to continue their mission, they were looking for similar contexts of larger cities and towns with good-sized Jewish populations and therefore a synagogue. Instead, God draws them to a place where they will need to reach out in a slightly different way. Again, they seek those who are open and eager to hear about the message they bring, but this time at a place of prayer and, later, in Athens – not only in the synagogue but also in the marketplace (17:17). It is possible that they already knew of the place of prayer, but the Greek suggests rather that they expected to find a place there and this would fit with suggestions in Philo and Josephus that there was a pattern of praying beside water.

So we see Paul, Silas and Timothy continuing to share the gospel, making connections with those who may be open, but finding them in a different context.

2 Faith, unity and hospitality

Acts 16:16–40

While we may expect that a number of people came to faith or encountered the Lord during the time that Paul and his companions were in Philippi, Luke chooses to recount in detail only three encounters, which were with people from very different social and cultural backgrounds. In yesterday's passage, Lydia (or possibly 'the Lydian', indicating her home area; 16:14) was a wealthy immigrant from Asia Minor, a businesswoman. The slave girl in today's passage is probably Greek and may well be from Philippi – there is nothing in the text to suggest she comes from elsewhere.

The Greek speaks of this girl being possessed by a python spirit. In classical mythology, pythons guarded the temple of Apollo and the Delphic oracle, and Apollo was said to inspire female devotees with the ability to predict the future. The slave girl is poor and powerless. Her owners use her for their own ends, rather than having any concern for her well-being. In crying out 'Most High God', she uses words that were used not only of God in the Psalms in the Septuagint, but also of Zeus, and so the words may not have been fully comprehensible or helpful. It may be partly concern for her well-being and Paul's awareness of the way that she was being used that leads to his annoyance in verse 18, understanding that if he allows her to continue following them and crying out, he, too, is in effect using her for his own ends.

The jailer, while probably not as well-off as Lydia, has status in his role and is likely a retired soldier and therefore Roman. It is probable that these three very different people are part of the beginning of the church in Philippi – called to become brothers and sisters (in verse 40 the Greek is *adelphoi* – 'brothers' rather than simply 'believers' as in TNIV).

With both Lydia and the jailer, their pattern of coming to faith includes baptism and hospitality. Lydia persuades Paul and his companions to stay with her (16:15), and the jailer is ready to take Paul and Silas into his home – providing food as well as washing their wounds (vv. 33–34). Paul and Silas are also ready to receive such practical hospitality from these new disciples, maybe making way for the partnership and relationship between Paul and the Philippians that is so evident in his letter to them.

3 Partnership in the gospel

In his opening prayer, Paul gives thanks for the Philippians' partnership or participation (*koinonia*) in the gospel – the word also means 'fellowship' and was used of business and marriage. At the same time, he reminds them of their share in the grace of God. They participate in the gospel and share in the grace of God in what they have received, but also partner with Paul in that same gospel endeavour. Paul probably has in mind the gift that the Philippians have sent him (4:15) and the practical sharing the Philippians have done to enable him in his gospel ministry. Paul will, however, go on to exhort them to live in such a way as to reflect the gospel (2:1–18) and so it seems likely that this *koinonia* in the gospel includes the Philippians' own sharing of the gospel in Philippi.

This partnership with Paul in the gospel is one that has led to a deep friendship, which is evidenced in Paul's opening greeting as well as in the prayer. Rather than note himself also as an apostle (compare Galatians 1:1; Romans 1:1; 1 Corinthians 1:1; 2 Corinthians 1:1), he writes solely as a *doulos*, a slave, of Christ Jesus. In using 'slave', he picks up the Greco-Roman usage of slaves of a master, as well as possibly the usage in the Septuagint of it to refer to servants of God. He does not major on his authority but speaks out of an established warm partnership. Paul and Timothy together are slaves of Jesus Christ – and the relationship with Jesus is the basis of the relationship and partnership between Paul, Timothy and the Philippians. In designating himself as a slave of Christ, Paul also points forward to the pattern of Christ's life (2:7) which he will go on to exhort the Philippians to follow.

As he speaks of his partnership with the Philippians, Paul may also be hinting at the partnership between the Philippians; he writes to *all* the saints (v. 1), of his feeling for *all* of them and the grace they *all* share in (v. 7), and of the way he longs for *all* of them (v. 8). In the context of tensions between individuals (e.g. Euodia and Syntyche; 4:2), this repeated use of 'all' may remind the Philippians of the fact that they together have a partnership with Paul and with one another in the gospel.

4 The priority of the gospel

Paul starts this section with a standard disclosure form, 'I want you to know that', which would often have been used in friendship letters to introduce information about the writer's own situation. However, we do not learn that much about Paul's situation, exactly what his situation in prison or chains is or in what way he is suffering. This may partially be because he expects Epaphroditus to inform them when he comes, but, more than that, Paul's priority for the Philippians is that they do not see his imprisonment or suffering as a negative thing, but rather that they see God at work through his situation. Paul presents himself as imprisoned for Christ – not simply because of his message, but for Christ, so that the gospel may advance in ways that it would otherwise not have done – through the palace guard hearing the good news and through others being encouraged to share the good news.

Some of this sharing is from negative motives – perhaps some see themselves as rival leaders to Paul, or perhaps their preaching is strongly anti-imperial as they try and hasten the end times, making it difficult for Paul. Whatever the reason, Paul does not accuse these people of sharing a false gospel, but rejoices in its sharing, so it seems unlikely that these people are related to the opponents who advocate circumcision for Gentiles (3:2). Instead, it seems more likely that they are people who in some way saw Paul as a rival and so preach hoping that he will get into more trouble as a result. However, as Frank Thielman notes, they are thwarted in their aim:

At the end of the day, after all their efforts to oppose Paul, they have only succeeded in doing the very thing that matters most to him and the thing his friends also do: They have preached Christ.

Thielman, p. 61

Paul's priority for the gospel is not only seen in his account of his imprisonment, but also in his reflection on his future and whether he will live or die. While Paul looks forward to being in Christ in death, his priority is not what he wants but what will most benefit the gospel, and therefore his reflection leads him to believe that he will continue to live and minister to the benefit of the gospel (and the Philippians).

5 Suffering citizens

Here, Paul turns from the disclosure form, where he informs the Philippians of the effects of his imprisonment and his priority for the gospel, to more of a letter of exhortation. He exhorts the Philippians to unity and courage in the face of opposition and suffering, addressing the fact that they are facing both internal tensions (4:2) and external opposition. As he does so, he uses a political term *politeuomai* – that is, 'live as citizens' or 'live out your citizenship'. For the inhabitants of Philippi, the fact that they were a Roman colony was a matter of pride, and being a Roman citizen brought status and privileges as well as expectations in terms of dress, customs and language. As Paul uses *politeuomai*, he plays on this idea of citizenship to remind them that while some of them may be Roman citizens in Philippi, their true citizenship is as a result of the gospel. The community of believers is a colony of the gospel, a colony of heaven, and they are to live accordingly.

As Paul encourages them in this, he also uses terms that were used in military contexts. They are to 'stand firm', a word used of soldiers at post. They are to be 'striving' together. There are 'those who oppose you'. In this, they are to be rooted in God and united with each other. They are to stand firm in 'one Spirit' – not here referring to a unity of people or *esprit de corps*, but rather unity in the Holy Spirit – and they are to be striving with 'one soul', united to their fellow believers.

As with Paul's suffering, the Philippians' suffering is for or on behalf of Christ, and Paul links it to his experience while he was with them and to his current situation, where suffering for Christ has led to the advancement of the gospel. They are not to be frightened by those who oppose them, for they are citizens of heaven and, as Paul has already demonstrated, God is at work in every circumstance. This lack of fearfulness will itself witness to those who are opposing them and be a sign of the fact that they are citizens of heaven and will be saved by God.

6 Christ-formed minds

Having already used the idea of citizenship to remind the Philippians of who they are and how they should see themselves, Paul continues to address how the Philippians should see things as he uses the word *phroneō* (vv. 2, 5), which can mean to think, to form or to hold an opinion. The Philippians are to think, to see things, to form their opinions in the way Christ does. They are to have Christ-formed minds. This is based in the fact that they are united with Christ, and this relationship and unity should lead them to become like Christ in the way they view things and therefore also in the way they act. As Paul exhorts them to have Christlike minds, he includes patterns of thinking and behaving which, if followed, will deal with the tensions in the Philippian church that Paul hints at throughout his letter.

Their relationships with one another are to be rooted in the same pattern of thinking and behaving that they see in Jesus:

- Jesus, who did not *harpagmos* equality with God (v. 6; *harpagmos* is a tricky word to translate, as it only occurs here in the New Testament; rather than meaning grasping at something, as some translations have it, it has the sense of not using something you have to your own advantage). Jesus becomes poor for our sakes (2 Corinthians 8:9).
- Jesus, who made himself nothing (v. 7; *keno*, sometimes translated 'emptying', used by Paul four other times in the New Testament and in each case it's used not of literally emptying but of metaphorically making something of no account).
- Jesus, who took the very nature of a slave (v. 7) and washed his disciples' feet (John 13).
- Jesus, who humbled himself to the point of death (v. 8) and who in the garden of Gethsemane said, 'Not my will, but yours' (Luke 22:42).

Unity with Christ should lead to unity with one another as they pattern their lives with one another on the example of Jesus. Being formed in Christ and his way of humility is integral to our proclamation of him as Lord.

Guidelines

- Paul, Silas and Timothy spend some time knowing where they are not meant to go before God reveals their destination in Paul's dream. How is God guiding you at the moment? How easy do you find it to keep following when you do not know exactly where you are going?

- Both Lydia and the jailer respond to the good news with faith and hospitality – what place does hospitality have in your life? In the life of your church? In how you evangelise? In your expectations of new disciples?

- Paul clearly rejoices in his relationship and partnership with the Philippians. Who do you partner with in the gospel where you are now? Take the opportunity to rejoice and give thanks for them.

- In Paul's introductory prayer, he prays for the Philippians to grow in love, knowledge, discernment and holiness. How do you pray for the Christians around you?

- Paul encourages the Philippians to live lives worthy of the gospel and gives them the example of Jesus. Where is God calling you to look and live more like Jesus? Do you know the unity with Christ, the comfort from his love, the common sharing in the Spirit that Paul sees as the ground and motivation for this Christlike living?

1 Christlike living: shining like stars

Philippians 2:12–18

Given the fact that Philippi was a Roman colony and worship of the emperor and other idols was expected, it would have been easy for the Philippians to try to hide in a corner. After all, they knew the risks: Paul and Silas had been beaten and thrown into prison and Paul hints in his letter at ongoing challenges for the Philippians. However, Paul's exhortation of them to have Christ-formed minds and lives is not simply something for their relationships with one another, for the community of believers; it is also for their outward relationships – they are to be witnesses in how they live.

This Christlike living is not dependent on Paul's presence, but on God at work within them and their living out of what God is doing. Paul's use of 'shine among them like stars in the sky' (v. 15) picks up language and ideas from Daniel 12:3, where 'those who lead many to righteousness' will shine 'like the stars for ever and ever'.

Christlike living, shining like stars, will be seen in how they relate to one another and those outside – not grumbling or arguing (v. 14), which may pick up the idea of the Israelites, having been brought out from slavery, grumbling in the wilderness. The Philippians are to live out their salvation – the way they have been brought out of slavery – not following the example of the Israelites, who grumbled and argued, but rather in the unity and Christlike relationships of 2:1–11. The way they do relationships will be a visible witness in the world in which they live. They are to be *amōma*, often translated 'pure', literally 'blameless' – not necessarily that they will be without sin, but that their behaviour should not be a stumbling block for those outside the church.

Their Christlike living involves holding out the word of life. *Epechontes* (from *epechō*) could mean to hold fast to the word of life, keeping it safe, but it could also mean to hold out the word of life in the sense of it being something they have but are also holding out for others to receive. This latter meaning seems more likely both because of the word order and because of the imagery, which echoes Daniel 12, where we see people come to be part of the believing community.

2 Christlike living: Timothy and Epaphroditus

Philippians 2:19–30

Having exhorted the Philippians to Christlike living within the Christian community and in the context of Philippian society, Paul gives the Philippians two examples of such Christlike living and Christ-formed minds: Timothy and Epaphroditus, two people who, like Jesus, are ready to serve others despite the cost to themselves.

Epaphroditus is ready to put the needs of others before his own; he travelled with the Philippian gift to Paul, and travel was often a risky business in the ancient world. He cared for Paul's needs – possibly simply by transporting the gift, but more probably in his companionship and care once he arrived with the gift, given how Paul speaks of the time that Epaphroditus has been with him. Epaphroditus' service has come at a cost – he has been ill, almost to the point of death. Maybe he picked up something while travelling, but in any case he has been suffering away from his main family and friends. Epaphroditus' worry for the Philippians is part of his concern for others – he is distressed that they may be worrying about him. Paul also describes Epaphroditus as a fellow-soldier, picking up the military language of 1:27–30 and pointing to the danger that Epaphroditus has faced and his common work in living out the gospel. In verse 29, when Paul speaks of Epaphroditus risking his life, he uses a word used by gamblers – in some ways Epaphroditus gambled with his life not only in travelling, but also in associating with Paul in chains.

While it includes less detail, Paul's praise of Timothy is likewise about his genuine concern for the welfare of others. Timothy's concern is not for his own interests, but for the interests of Jesus Christ.

By giving Timothy and Epaphroditus as examples of what he has been talking about, Paul also demonstrates the way his mind and behaviour have been formed by Christ: rather than hold on to the companionship and help of Timothy and Epaphroditus (both of whom he obviously holds dear), he is ready to send them to the Philippians for their benefit despite the cost to himself.

3 Confidence and knowing Jesus

Philippians 3:1–14

In what or whom do you trust? Paul had lots of credentials he could trust in. He could tick the Jewish credential boxes – ceremony, ancestry, learning, zeal and faithfulness to the law – but he does not. It is not simply that he does not put his trust in them, but also that he considers them all loss, all garbage, compared to the surpassing worth of knowing Christ. It is in knowing Christ that Paul's trust and confidence lies – that is his foundation. We know that Paul continued to use his background – we see it in his knowledge and quoting of the Old Testament and in the way he uses his Roman citizenship (e.g. Acts 16:37) – but where he had come from and what he had achieved were nothing compared to knowing Jesus.

As Paul addresses the internal challenges for the Philippian church in terms of tension as well as the opposition they were facing internally, he warns them against putting their confidence in anything apart from

Jesus – whether their own background or outward signs like circumcision (or maybe even their own following of Paul's instructions in Philippians 2). Whether the 'mutilators of the flesh' (v. 2) are non-Christian Jews or Jewish Christians seeking to persuade Gentile Christians to be circumcised is not clear. However, Paul is clear in his warning not to put confidence in physical circumcision. Instead of circumcision, *peritomē* (to cut around), Paul uses *katatomē* (cut to pieces; mutilate), and he reserves *peritomē* for those whose confidence and boasting is in Christ Jesus.

Paul's confidence is in Jesus and in knowing him, which Paul places over and above anything else. This knowing is relational, but much more than simply a relationship. This knowing Christ involves:

- being right with God because of being united with Jesus – having righteousness through faith in Jesus Christ.
- knowing Jesus as Lord – the one whom God has exalted to the highest place, whose name is above every name, at whose name every knee should bow.
- participation in the resurrection as well as in the sufferings of Jesus. Paul has already written about suffering for Christ (1:29) and reminded the Philippians that they are following Jesus, the one whose pattern of life includes self-giving to the point of death (2:8).
- ultimate life and knowing Jesus' resurrection and its power both now and in the age to come.

Knowing Jesus draws Paul into God's purposes – Christ's purpose in taking hold of him (v. 12) and Paul's participation in that purpose.

4 Citizens of heaven

Philippians 3:15–21

Having written of his own mindset of considering everything loss compared to knowing Jesus and his goal of straining towards the prize, Paul encourages the Philippians to follow his example (v. 17) and to live out the truth that their citizenship is in heaven (v. 20). The word he uses in verse 16 translated 'live up to' (*stoicheō*) is relatively rare in the New Testament. It is used in Romans 4:12 when speaking of the life of faith; in Galatians 5:22–25 of the life characterised by the fruit of the Spirit; and in Galatians 6:15–16 of boasting only in Jesus Christ as new creations. In wider literature, it is used of a group of people being in a line or of being in line with a person or a way of living, and so continues the idea of behaviour being in line with Christ.

Paul urges the Philippians to imitate him rather than to be drawn to the pattern of those who are enemies of the cross of Christ. This seems to be a different group from the mutilators referred to in 3:2. They may be those who try to add things to the cross, or possibly those who do not accept the way Jesus fulfilled his calling and who reject the pattern of the cross-shaped life for their own lives – those whose focus is on their own interests and freedoms rather than on the interests of Jesus and those around them. In contrast to their focus on their own ends, Paul calls the Philippians to imitate his example, which he has pointed them to elsewhere in the letter – the way he faced persecution and suffering (1:13), the way he had confidence in Christ Jesus (1:20–21), the way he is focused on knowing Jesus (3:7–11).

While Paul has earlier reminded the Philippians that they are part of a colony of heaven in Philippi, here Paul uses the idea of being citizens of heaven to include both the present (a present way of living in contrast to that of the enemies of the cross) and a future certainty (Jesus' return and the ultimate consummation).

5 Christlike living: unity and peace

Philippians 4:1–9

Here, Paul returns to ideas from 1:27–30 and applies them more specifically to the Philippian congregation. They are to stand firm (1:27; 4:1). They are to be working together and of one mind (1:27; 2:2; 4:2) – a unity which is not just a theory but is to be worked out practically in relationship. While Paul is addressing discord within the congregation, it is clear that his warmth for the Philippians continues – in verse 1 he twice calls them 'beloved'. Indeed, his affection for them is evident throughout the letter. He pleads with Euodia and Syntyche, but he does so from a place of honouring them and their role as co-workers in the gospel. While *syzygos* (v. 3) could be the name of the person who Paul urges to help them, this seems less likely as it is not attested as a proper name elsewhere. Rather, Paul urges this co-worker/yokefellow to assist the two in becoming united as they respond to all that he has already written to them.

The future certainty that Paul pointed towards at the end of chapter 3 continues to undergird his practical exhortations here. Paul refers to the

Philippians as his joy and crown, picking up the idea of the crown an athlete could win at the end of a race and the prize that he is running for (3:12–14). He also reminds the Philippians that the Lord is near (v. 5), using the adverb formed from the verb that Jesus uses of the kingdom being near (Matthew 4:17), which can mean both near and coming. In doing so, Paul points to the confidence they can have in the Lord's presence with them, as well as to the future hope they have of Jesus not only appearing from heaven but also bringing all things under his control (3:20–21).

Running through the passage is the idea of peace:

- being at peace with one another and standing firm and united.
- knowing peace in the everyday challenges of life and the specific challenges in terms of opposition to Christian faith in Philippi, because the Philippians can entrust their concerns and situations to the Lord, who is near.
- seeking peace by focusing on what is true, good and lovely, rather than focusing on the challenges, concerns and opposition, which he has just encouraged them to entrust to the Lord.

6 Christlike living: giving and receiving

Philippians 4:10–23

Throughout the letter, the close and warm relationship between Paul and the Philippians has been evident. This close relationship is also seen in Paul's willingness to receive from the Philippians, given the fact that he refused help from the Corinthians. In this final section of the letter, Paul acknowledges the gift the Philippians have sent him with Epaphroditus. He is clearly glad to have received it and is in effect saying thank you (without actually saying the words), but he does so very carefully.

There are several reasons why Paul is careful about who he receives money from and how. First, he does not want to be seen as one of the travelling philosophers who were dependent on gifts of money and therefore were sometimes seen in a bad light and could be influenced by their benefactors. Second, the norms of patronage in the Greco-Roman world meant that gifts were expected to be repaid either by gifts of a similar value or by flattery. Paul does not want to be under the influence or authority of those he is seeking to share the good news of Jesus with, which might make him feel pressured to change his message. Third, giving thanks might give the impression that he wants the Philippians to send more, and Paul does not want to make the Philippians feel obligated to send further gifts.

Therefore, Paul is very careful to say that he is content. He was content before the gift arrived and he does not need more now that he has it. He writes to the Philippians of how he has learned to be content in every situation, content not because of what he has or does not have, nor because of his strength, but content because of Jesus. He is not self-sufficient, as was the aim of the Stoics (who sought to live with few things and be unaffected by pain or pleasure), but God-sufficient.

Paul also focuses on the relationship and partnership between himself and the Philippians – they have shared in giving and receiving over time. It is a deep, three-way relationship rooted in Jesus, so that the gift they have given is in effect given to God. Therefore God will in turn supply their needs, rather than Paul being responsible for a return gift. While Paul and the Philippians act out the giving and receiving, it is God who is the provider, the giver, the source of all good gifts (James 1:17).

Guidelines

- Paul encourages the Philippians to work out their salvation with fear and trembling, so that they may shine likes stars holding out the word of life. He gives them the practical examples of not grumbling or arguing. What difference would it make to your life and witness if you did not grumble or argue? In what ways does your life and the life of your church mean that you shine like stars as you hold out the word of life in the place where you live/work?

- Paul shows how Timothy and Epaphroditus are practical examples of putting the interests of others first (as Paul himself does in choosing to send both of them to the Philippians). Where do you see examples of such caring around you?

- Paul considers everything a loss compared to knowing Christ. What might God be calling you to consider a loss? What does knowing Christ mean for you?

- Paul encourages the Philippians to follow his example. Whose example of faith are you following? Who is following your example of faith?

- 'Do not be anxious about anything, but in every situation, by prayer and petition, with thanksgiving, present your requests to God' (4:6). How do you pray about your daily life? How might Paul's words encourage you in your prayer?

- As Paul acknowledges the gift from the Philippians, he places it within the picture of God being the ultimate provider and describes the relationship and partnership between him and the Philippians as being three-way, including God. How easy do you find it to trust in God for his provision? Where have you seen God's provision for you and who has been part of it? How easy do you find it to be content, in the way that Paul describes? Where are you called to be part of God's provision for others?

FURTHER READING

Gordon D. Fee, *Paul's Letter to the Philippians* (Eerdmans, 1995).

Joseph Hellerman, *Embracing Shared Ministry: Power and status in the early church and why it matters today* (Kregel, 2013).

G. W. Peterman, *Paul's Gift from Philippi: Conventions of gift exchange and Christian giving* (CUP, 1997).

Frank Thielman, *Philippians (The NIV Application Commentary)* (Zondervan, 1995).

Steve Walton, 'Paul, patronage and pay: what do we know about the apostle's financial support?' in Trevor J. Burke and Brian S. Rosner (eds), *Paul as Missionary: Identity, activity, theology, and practice* (T&T Clark, 2011), pp. 220–33.

Overleaf... Guidelines forthcoming issue | Author profile |
Recommended reading | Order and subscription forms

Guidelines forthcoming issue

HELEN PAYNTER

Our next set of notes will take us from September into Advent and Christmas. I'm excited by the notes that we have to offer. Let me offer some highlights to whet your appetite.

For Advent, David Kerrigan has given us two weeks of notes on what the gospel of peace looks like in a world of wars. As always, David is helpfully reflective as he invites us to grapple with some of the breadth of the gospel's implications in our broken world. Also very challenging is Andy Angel's latest set of readings on Matthew. Andy helps us to understand the bold and forthright challenge that Jesus presents, as he takes us through the next few chapters of the gospel. It doesn't always make for comfortable reading, which is entirely fitting!

We will also be providing more thoughts about what the age-old truths and imperatives of the kingdom look like in our own generation. In an age when there is a great deal written on church leadership, not all of it well-founded on biblical and theological principles, Rosie Button has written a thoughtful set of reflections about leadership in a changing world, drawn from the life and writings of the apostle Paul. I have also very much enjoyed reading Kate Bruce's reflections on deep spirituality and how it might shape our mission in the twenty-first century. I appreciate not only the challenging perspectives that Kate offers, but also the really beautiful way that she writes. I'm sure that the poets among our readers will particularly value her contribution. To complement this, we have two weeks of readings that grapple with the cosmic scope of salvation from the familiar and well-loved pen of Derek Tidball.

As someone who works in a theological college and believes passionately in the value of training the minds of future ministers, as well as their hearts and hands, I was delighted to read Helen Morris' contribution for the next issue. Helen is a New Testament specialist based at Moorlands, and she brings us a very stimulating set of readings showcasing some of the new insights that can emerge from the biblical text when contemporary scholarly techniques are applied to it. If anyone needs persuasion of it, Helen's notes are proof of the value of deep study and, indeed, of ongoing academic research into the Bible. We also have a new writer next month, Terry Griffith, who will be taking us through the sometimes neglected Johannine letters in a helpful fortnight of reflections.

September, for many of us, is more the start of the new year than January. Some of us will be returning to a new academic year, and others will be seeing children or grandchildren starting new school or university adventures. For most of us, the summer holidays mark the longest break that we have, and therefore we return in September with a sense of being rested and perhaps having new plans. As you gear up for whatever new things the autumn might bring, I hope that you will find our next edition of *Guidelines* to be a provocative and inspiring companion.

Why the Bible matters to me: Peter Hatton

Oh Book! Infinite sweetnesse! let my heart
Suck ev'ry letter and a hony gain…

So begins one of George Herbert's poems on the scriptures. Those who might have expected something complex and cerebral when Herbert (1593–1633), an academic theologian by training, talks about the Bible will be confounded by the physicality of these words, particularly how the stress falls on 'suck' in the second line. He is, of course, prompted by scripture itself; most obviously Psalm 119:103, which the Authorised Version renders 'How sweet are thy words unto my taste! yea, sweeter than honey to my mouth.'

This is not the only place where the word of God (which includes but is not limited to the written word) is described as 'food' (e.g Isaiah 55:2; Hebrews 5:12). There are, of course, other pictures offered to us: the word is a 'sword' (Ephesians 6:17, Hebrews 4:12); it is like 'refined silver and gold' (Psalm 12:2); the very 'breath of God' (2 Timothy 3:16). However, the notion that the word of God disclosed in scripture is something as necessary to life as food is a profound and, indeed, a troubling one. It implies that if individual believers, churches and – indeed, I would argue, nations – are deprived of this word, they grow weak, starve and die.

Psalm 119's precise comparison with a certain sort of food – namely, honey – is perhaps, particularly telling. For, let me tell you, as the husband

143

(and, under strict supervision, occasional helper) of a beekeeper, the sweetness of honey is won only by constant care, much labour, great wisdom and, occasionally, by pain (bees have stings!). Modern people whose food and drink are sweetened by refined sugar, or even by saccharine, are liable to misread talk of the word being sweet. We may, accordingly, expect the written word to be already so processed that there is nothing in it that is sour or harsh.

We are then confused when we open our Bibles and find in them many passages that are not, on the face of it, sweetness and light. However, when the word rebukes, challenges, puzzles, even offends its readers, this is not a sign that it is not nourishing. Rather, such unpalatable passages cry out for us to work on them until they disclose their hidden delights.

Psalm 1:2 speaks of the blessings of the one who delights in 'God's law'. That person 'meditates on it day and night'; but the Hebrew word used here is also used in Isaiah 31:4 of a lion 'growling' over its prey. So the verse suggests not some mystical, intellectual experience but rather how the satisfaction of a great hunger might prompt us to exult as we eat, to say 'yum, yum'. I will not pretend that that is what I always say when I read my Bible! However, again and again I have been moved to praise its author when the written word has met my needs, needs as deep as hunger, urgent as thirst.

An extract from *How to Read the Bible*

How to read the Bible? And how to apply it? To read and engage with the Bible, we first need to understand the story, the styles of writing and the approaches we find in the text. Michael Parsons encourages readers to look at the whole biblical storyline before demonstrating ways of approaching individual texts. Topics include understanding different genres, the importance of narrative, imaginative reading, praying the Bible, difficult passages and what to do with them, and how to apply scripture to our own lives.

The following is an edited extract from the chapter 'Why do we read the Bible?'

For some years now, I've read the Bible every twelve months or so. Beginning with the Psalms, I read the rest in a certain order, in lengthy portions, getting to know what the book is about. This, in itself, is useful, of course. However, this is what Eugene Peterson would term 'reading', not 'listening'. It's a good thing to do, but, as we've seen, it won't gain the desired purpose of scripture, which is for us to become mature in Christ, to know him in resurrection power and in suffering. To listen, I need to pause and contemplate the text, to pray through it, to reflect on the experience of God – Israel's or the writer's and my own – seeking to see the words as enculturated in the period of their composition, but somehow, through the wonderful present work of the Holy Spirit, applied to my own time and situation. To listen to scripture, I need to grasp something of the central importance of Jesus Christ to the narrative and to my own life and well-being. And, I would say, I need to grasp the importance of experiencing God through the Spirit as he informs my thinking and forms my life to exhibit something of Christ himself. It happens on a different level than merely reading scripture; it is 'listening to', or 'engaging with', scripture.

In his later work on the subject, *Eat This Book*, Eugene Peterson speaks of God revealing himself to us through the text of scripture as we 'listen', pulling us into the revelation and welcoming us as participants in it: 'God's word is written, handed down, and translated for us so that we can enter the plot.' This is an important point. It perhaps reminds us of the active word in Peter Phillips' image of the Bible as an engine – an engine driving us to recognise the God behind the words. But Peterson is speaking about the narrative of scripture, the story of God's people throughout biblical history (Old Testament and New), into which we are drawn by God's revelation to us through the witness of scripture. It reminds me of a fascinating study of tradition by Delwin Brown. Speaking of the curatorial character of tradition, he says it has force; it's experienced as some kind of distinctive pull. Employing an image, Brown speaks of it as more like a galaxy than a planet. The planet, he says, is static in its 'brute given-ness'; the galaxy, in contrast, functionally exerts its own gravitational pull, 'a kind of inner drive', with its ragged edges and its inner swirl. This seems reminiscent of much of what Peterson says about biblical narrative. If we 'listen' to it, it pulls us in, it has its own gravitational pull, 'a kind of inner drive'. And, as we enter the narrative of scripture, we work out who we are, our roots; we negotiate our own identity – it's a very personal thing.

It's a personal experience because it involves primarily the God of revelation and us, those who listen to or engage with his compelling voice. Eugene Peterson helpfully puts it this way:

But here's the thing: every aspect, every form is personal – God is relational at the core – and so whatever is said, whatever is revealed, whatever is received is also personal and relational… The corollary to this is that I, because I am a person, am personally involved in the revelation. Every word I hear, everything I see in my imagination as the story unfolds, involves me relationally, pulls me into participation, matters to my core identity, affects who I am and what I do.

Why read the Bible? Because in reading, or rather 'listening', to use Peterson's helpful distinction, we listen for God's voice, his revelation to which the Bible is a faithful witness. We do so, of course, through other people's experiences of God and his salvation, and sometimes through their experiences of God's apparent absence. So, it's not always going to be easy reading/listening! Indeed, at times it is difficult to glean the Lord's voice at all. But we read in the hope and the confidence that because he is personal, his purpose for us is good. We read so that we might enter the storyline or narrative plot and be transformed little by little into the image of his precious son. We need to keep this in mind as we turn later to some strategies for reading the pages of scripture; we don't want to learn to read only to miss the divine art and purpose of listening.

To order a copy of this book, please use the order form on page 149 or visit **brfonline.org.uk**.

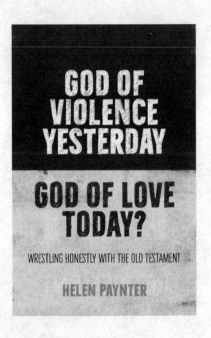

While acknowledging that there are no easy answers, in *God of Violence Yesterday, God of Love Today?*, Helen Paynter faces the tough questions head-on and offers a fresh, accessible approach to a significant issue. For all those seeking to engage with the Bible and gain confidence in the God it portrays, she provides tools for reading and interpreting biblical texts, and points to ways of dealing with the overall trajectories of violence.

God of Violence Yesterday, God of Love Today?
Wrestling honestly with the Old Testament
Helen Paynter
978 0 85746 639 6   £9.99
brfonline.org.uk

To order

Online: **brfonline.org.uk**
Telephone: +44 (0)1865 319700
Mon–Fri 9.15–17.30

Delivery times within the UK are normally 15 working days. Prices are correct at the time of going to press but may change without prior notice.

Title	Price	Qty	Total
Holy Habits Bible Reflections: Biblical Teaching, Fellowship, Breaking Bread, Prayer, Sharing Resources, Serving, Eating Together, Gladness and Generosity, Worship and Making More Disciples (*delete as appropriate)	£3.99 each		
Holy Habits Group Studies: Biblical Teaching, Fellowship, Breaking Bread, Prayer, Sharing Resources, Serving, Eating Together, Gladness and Generosity, Worship and Making More Disciples (*delete as appropriate)	£6.99 each		
How to Read the Bible	£8.99		
Make the Most of Retirement	£7.99		
God of Violence Yesterday, God of Love Today?	£9.99		

POSTAGE AND PACKING CHARGES			
Order value	UK	Europe	Rest of world
Under £7.00	£2.00	Available on request	Available on request
£7.00–£29.99	£3.00		
£30.00 and over	FREE		

Total value of books	
Postage and packing	
Total for this order	

Please complete in BLOCK CAPITALS

Title .... First name/initials .... Surname.......................................

Address...

.... Postcode ....

Acc. No. .... Telephone ....

Email..

Method of payment

❑ Cheque (made payable to BRF) ❑ MasterCard / Visa

Card no. ☐☐☐☐ ☐☐☐☐ ☐☐☐☐ ☐☐☐☐ ☐☐☐☐ ☐☐☐☐

Expires end [M][M] [Y][Y] Security code* ☐☐☐ Last 3 digits on the reverse of the card

Signature* .... Date .... /............ /............
*ESSENTIAL IN ORDER TO PROCESS YOUR ORDER

Please return this form to:
BRF, 15 The Chambers, Vineyard, Abingdon OX14 3FE | **enquiries@brf.org.uk**
To read our terms and find out about cancelling your order, please visit **brfonline.org.uk/terms**.

The Bible Reading Fellowship (BRF) is a Registered Charity (233280)

BRF needs you!

If you're one of our regular *Guidelines* readers, you will know all about the benefits and blessings of regular Bible study and the value of serious daily notes to guide, inform and challenge you.

Here are some recent comments from *Guidelines* readers:

'... *very thoughtful and spiritually helpful. [These notes] are speaking to the church as it is today, and therefore to Christians like us who live in today's world.*'

'*You have assembled an amazingly diverse group of people and their contributions are most certainly thoughtful.*'

If you have similarly positive things to say about *Guidelines*, would you be willing to share your experience with others? Could you ask for a brief slot during church notices or write a short piece for your church magazine or website? Do you belong to groups, formal or informal, academic or professional, where you could share your experience of using *Guidelines* and encourage others to try them?

It doesn't need to be complicated: just answering these three questions in what you say or write will get your message across:

- How do *Guidelines* Bible study notes help you grow in knowledge and faith?
- Where, when and how do you use them?
- What would you say to people who haven't yet tried them?

We can supply further information if you need it and would love to hear about it if you do give a talk or write an article.

For more information:

- Email **enquiries@brf.org.uk**
- Telephone BRF on +44 (0)1865 319700 Mon–Fri 9.15–17.30
- Write to us at BRF, 15 The Chambers, Vineyard, Abingdon OX14 3FE

Enabling all ages to grow in faith

At BRF, we long for people of all ages to grow in faith and understanding of the Bible. That's what all our work as a charity is about.

- Our **Living Faith** range of resources helps Christians go deeper in their understanding of scripture, in prayer and in their walk with God. Our conferences and events bring people together to share this journey.

- We also want to make it easier for local churches to engage effectively in ministry and mission – by helping them bring new families into a growing relationship with God through **Messy Church** or by supporting churches as they nurture the spiritual life of older people through **Anna Chaplaincy**.

- Our **Holy Habits** resources help whole congregations grow together as disciples of Jesus, living out and sharing their faith.

- Our **Parenting for Faith** team coaches parents and others to raise God-connected children and teens, and enables churches to fully support them.

- We also offer a professional education service, **Barnabas in Schools**, giving primary schools confidence, expertise and opportunities for exploring Christianity in creative ways that engage all pupils.

Do you share our vision?

Though a significant proportion of BRF's funding is generated through our charitable activities, we are dependent on the generous support of individuals, churches and charitable trusts.

If you share our vision, would you help us to enable even more people of all ages to grow in faith? Your prayers and financial support are vital for the work that we do. You could:

- Support BRF's ministry with a regular donation;
- Support us with a one-off gift;
- Consider leaving a gift to BRF in your will (see page 152);
- Encourage your church to support BRF as part of your church's giving to home mission – perhaps focusing on a specific ministry or programme;
- Most important of all, support BRF with your prayers.

Donate at **brf.org.uk/donate** or use the form on pages 153–54.

Making an impact

If someone asked you who throughout history (excluding Jesus) has left the biggest impact, what would be your answer?

For some, it may be Albert Einstein, who is responsible for developing the theory of relativity, came up with the formula $E = mc^2$ and in 1921 received the Nobel Prize in Physics.

For those who love to read, it may be someone like Johannes Gutenberg who, in 1439, invented the printing press.

Or maybe the person who has left the biggest impact, in your opinion, is someone who is close to you, whose name isn't widely known but whose contribution to your life is valuable.

Here at BRF, we have many people who contribute in such a way. They are people whose names are not widely known, but to us they are heroes.

It is because of these heroes – their willingness to partner with us and their financial gift – that we can continue inspiring and equipping future generations to grow in faith. Through access to our notes, books and creative programmes, people are encountering Jesus and lives are being impacted.

If you would like to partner with us, and the time is ever right for you to remember a charity in your will, please remember BRF.

For further information about making a gift to BRF in your will, please visit **brf.org.uk/lastingdifference**, contact us at **+44 (0)1865 319700** or email **giving@brf.org.uk**.

Whatever you can do or give, we thank you for your support.

Pray. Give. Get involved.
brf.org.uk

SHARING OUR VISION – MAKING A GIFT

I would like to make a gift to support BRF. Please use my gift for:

☐ BRF charity ☐ Barnabas in Schools ☐ Parenting for Faith
☐ Messy Church ☐ Anna Chaplaincy ☐ where it is most needed

Title	First name/initials	Surname
Address		
		Postcode
Email		
Telephone		
Signature		Date

giftaid it You can add an extra 25p to every £1 you give.

Please treat as Gift Aid donations all qualifying gifts of money made

☐ today, ☐ in the past four years, ☐ and in the future.

I am a UK taxpayer and understand that if I pay less Income Tax and/or Capital Gains Tax in the current tax year than the amount of Gift Aid claimed on all my donations, it is my responsibility to pay any difference.

☐ My donation does not qualify for Gift Aid.

Please notify BRF if you want to cancel this Gift Aid declaration, change your name or home address, or no longer pay sufficient tax on your income and/or capital gains.

Please complete other side of form ➡

Please return this form to:
BRF, 15 The Chambers, Vineyard, Abingdon OX14 3FE

BRF

The Bible Reading Fellowship is a Registered Charity (233280)

SHARING OUR VISION – MAKING A GIFT

Regular giving

By Direct Debit: You can set up a Direct Debit quickly and easily at **brf.org.uk/donate**

By Standing Order: Please contact our Fundraising Administrator +44 (0)1865 319700 | **giving@brf.org.uk**

One-off donation

Please accept my gift of:

☐ £10 ☐ £50 ☐ £100 Other £ ☐

by (*delete as appropriate*):

☐ Cheque/Charity Voucher payable to 'BRF'

☐ MasterCard/Visa/Debit card/Charity card

Name on card

Card no. ☐☐☐☐ ☐☐☐☐ ☐☐☐☐ ☐☐☐☐

Expires end ☐M☐M ☐Y☐Y Security code* ☐☐☐

*Last 3 digits on the reverse of the card
ESSENTIAL IN ORDER TO PROCESS YOUR PAYMENT

Signature Date

☐ I would like to leave a gift in my will to BRF.

For more information, visit **brf.org.uk/lastingdifference**

For help or advice regarding making a gift, please contact our Fundraising Administrator +44 (0)1865 319700

◖ Please complete other side of form
Please return this form to:
BRF, 15 The Chambers, Vineyard, Abingdon OX14 3FE

BRF

The Bible Reading Fellowship is a Registered Charity (233280)

GL0220

GUIDELINES SUBSCRIPTION RATES

Please note our new subscription rates, current until 30 April 2021:

Individual subscriptions
covering 3 issues for under 5 copies, payable in advance
(including postage & packing):

	UK	Europe	Rest of world
Guidelines 1-year subscription	£17.85	£25.80	£29.70
Guidelines 3-year subscription (9 issues)	£50.85	N/A	N/A

Group subscriptions
covering 3 issues for 5 copies or more, sent to one UK address (post free):

Guidelines 1-year subscription	£14.10 per set of 3 issues p.a.

Please note that the annual billing period for group subscriptions runs from
1 May to 30 April.

Overseas group subscription rates
Available on request. Please email **enquiries@brf.org.uk**.

Copies may also be obtained from Christian bookshops:

Guidelines	£4.70 per copy

All our Bible reading notes can be ordered
online by visiting **brfonline.org.uk/collections/
subscriptions**

GUIDELINES

Guidelines is also available as
an app for Android, iPhone and iPad
brfonline.org.uk/collections/apps

All our Bible reading notes can be ordered online by visiting
brfonline.org.uk/collections/subscriptions

☐ I would like to take out a subscription:

Title _____ First name/initials _____ Surname _____

Address _____

_____ Postcode _____

Telephone _____ Email _____

Please send *Guidelines* beginning with the September 2020 / January 2021 /
May 2021 issue (*delete as appropriate*):

(*please tick box*)	UK	Europe	Rest of world
Guidelines 1-year subscription	☐ £17.85	☐ £25.80	☐ £29.70
Guidelines 3-year subscription	☐ £50.85	N/A	N/A

Total enclosed £ _____ (cheques should be made payable to 'BRF')

Please charge my MasterCard / Visa ☐ Debit card ☐ with £ _____

Card no. ☐☐☐☐ ☐☐☐☐ ☐☐☐☐ ☐☐☐☐

Expires end ☐☐ ☐☐   Security code* ☐☐☐   Last 3 digits on the reverse
of the card

Signature* _____ Date _____ /_____ /_____

*ESSENTIAL IN ORDER TO PROCESS YOUR PAYMENT

To set up a Direct Debit, please also complete the Direct Debit instruction
on page 159 and return it to BRF with this form.

Please return this form to:
BRF, 15 The Chambers, Vineyard, Abingdon OX14 3FE

To read our terms and find out about cancelling your order, please visit **brfonline.org.uk/terms**.

The Bible Reading Fellowship (BRF) is a Registered Charity (233280)

GUIDELINES GIFT SUBSCRIPTION FORM

☐ I would like to give a gift subscription (please provide both names and addresses):

Title _____ First name/initials _____ Surname _____

Address _____

_____ Postcode _____

Telephone _____ Email _____

Gift subscription name _____

Gift subscription address _____

_____ Postcode _____

Gift message (20 words max. or include your own gift card):

_____

_____

Please send *Guidelines* beginning with the September 2020 / January 2021 / May 2021 issue (*delete as appropriate*):

(please tick box)	UK	Europe	Rest of world
Guidelines 1-year subscription	☐ £17.85	☐ £25.80	☐ £29.70
Guidelines 3-year subscription	☐ £50.85	N/A	N/A

Total enclosed £ _____ (cheques should be made payable to 'BRF')

Please charge my MasterCard / Visa ☐ Debit card ☐ with £ _____

Card no. ☐☐☐☐ ☐☐☐☐ ☐☐☐☐ ☐☐☐☐

Expires end ☐☐ ☐☐ Security code* ☐☐☐ Last 3 digits on the reverse of the card

Signature* _____ Date _____ /_____ /_____

*ESSENTIAL IN ORDER TO PROCESS YOUR PAYMENT

To set up a Direct Debit, please also complete the Direct Debit instruction on page 159 and return it to BRF with this form.

Please return this form to:
BRF, 15 The Chambers, Vineyard, Abingdon OX14 3FE

To read our terms and find out about cancelling your order, please visit **brfonline.org.uk/terms**.

The Bible Reading Fellowship (BRF) is a Registered Charity (233280)

DIRECT DEBIT PAYMENT

You can pay for your annual subscription to our Bible reading notes using Direct Debit. You need only give your bank details once, and the payment is made automatically every year until you cancel it. If you would like to pay by Direct Debit, please use the form opposite, entering your BRF account number under 'Reference number'.

You are fully covered by the Direct Debit Guarantee:

The Direct Debit Guarantee

- This Guarantee is offered by all banks and building societies that accept instructions to pay Direct Debits.
- If there are any changes to the amount, date or frequency of your Direct Debit, The Bible Reading Fellowship will notify you 10 working days in advance of your account being debited or as otherwise agreed. If you request The Bible Reading Fellowship to collect a payment, confirmation of the amount and date will be given to you at the time of the request.
- If an error is made in the payment of your Direct Debit, by The Bible Reading Fellowship or your bank or building society, you are entitled to a full and immediate refund of the amount paid from your bank or building society.
- If you receive a refund you are not entitled to, you must pay it back when The Bible Reading Fellowship asks you to.
- You can cancel a Direct Debit at any time by simply contacting your bank or building society. Written confirmation may be required. Please also notify us.

The Bible Reading Fellowship

Instruction to your bank or building society to pay by Direct Debit

Please fill in the whole form using a ballpoint pen and return it to:
BRF, 15 The Chambers, Vineyard, Abingdon OX14 3FE

Service User Number: | 5 | 5 | 8 | 2 | 2 | 9 |

Name and full postal address of your bank or building society

To: The Manager	Bank/Building Society
Address	
	Postcode

Name(s) of account holder(s)

Branch sort code

| | | – | | | – | | |

Bank/Building Society account number

| | | | | | | | |

Reference number

| | | | | | | | | | |

Instruction to your Bank/Building Society
Please pay The Bible Reading Fellowship Direct Debits from the account detailed
in this instruction, subject to the safeguards assured by the Direct Debit Guarantee.
I understand that this instruction may remain with The Bible Reading Fellowship
and, if so, details will be passed electronically to my bank/building society.

Signature(s)

Banks and Building Societies may not accept Direct Debit instructions for some
types of account.

Enabling all ages to grow in faith

Anna Chaplaincy
Barnabas in Schools
Holy Habits
Living Faith
Messy Church
Parenting for Faith

The Bible Reading Fellowship (BRF) is a Christian charity that resources individuals and churches and provides a professional education service to primary schools.

Our vision is to enable people of all ages to grow in faith and understanding of the Bible and to see more people equipped to exercise their gifts in leadership and ministry.

To find out more about our ministries and programmes, visit

brf.org.uk